IS YOUR
LIFE
MAPPED
OUT?

'I love this book! Dr. David Hamilton's brilliant, captivating book is a tour de force in discovering who you are and how you can shape your destiny. He's done what very few writers have ever achieved – he's successfully merged physics with metaphysics – and the result is truly remarkable.

'The depth of David's scientific perspective dovetails perfectly with his mystical awareness of the universe. This thought-provoking book will leave you with a deeper awe of your place in the cosmos. Highly recommended!'
Denise Linn, bestselling author of *Sacred Space*

'Is Your Life Mapped Out? *is inspiring. David's exploration of destiny, reality, and the human consciousness is powerful and steeped with insight. His reflections are personal and yet relatable. I learned from this book, and thoroughly enjoyed the process. Another fantastic accomplishment by David Hamilton.'
Ileen Maisel, Executive Producer of *The Golden Compass*

'We each have a map set out for our life. David brings science and spiritually together to show that we have an incredible level of untapped power and choice for how we unfold our life. We can create a new map for our life that is more affirming and exciting than we had ever realized.'
Nick Williams, author of eight books including *The Work We Were Born To Do* and cofounder of www.inspired-entrepreneur.com

'David's compassion for people and love for life is contagious! Creating a bridge between science and spirituality, there is no doubt this book will leave you filled with enthusiasm. The rich content brings you an understanding of WHO you are, WHAT you are capable of and HOW to create it. I trust this work will bring a real light to your life, and of course our dear planet. Enjoy! I certainly did!'
Kyle Gray, author of *The Angel Whisperer*

IS YOUR LIFE MAPPED OUT?

UNRAVELLING THE MYSTERY OF DESTINY VS FREE WILL

DAVID R. HAMILTON PhD

HAY HOUSE

Australia • Canada • Hong Kong • India
South Africa • United Kingdom • United States

First published and distributed in the United Kingdom by:
Hay House UK Ltd, 292B Kensal Rd, London W10 5BE.
Tel.: (44) 20 8962 1230; Fax: (44) 20 8962 1239.
www.hayhouse.co.uk

Published and distributed in the United States of America by:
Hay House, Inc., PO Box 5100, Carlsbad, CA 92018-5100.
Tel.: (1) 760 431 7695 or (800) 654 5126; Fax: (1) 760 431 6948 or (800) 650 5115.
www.hayhouse.com

Published and distributed in Australia by:
Hay House Australia Ltd, 18/36 Ralph St, Alexandria NSW 2015.
Tel.: (61) 2 9669 4299; Fax: (61) 2 9669 4144.
www.hayhouse.com.au

Published and distributed in the Republic of South Africa by:
Hay House SA (Pty), Ltd, PO Box 990, Witkoppen 2068.
Tel./Fax: (27) 11 467 8904. www.hayhouse.co.za

Published and distributed in India by:
Hay House Publishers India, Muskaan Complex, Plot No.3, B-2,
Vasant Kunj, New Delhi – 110 070. Tel.: (91) 11 4176 1620; Fax: (91) 11 4176 1630.
www.hayhouse.co.in

Distributed in Canada by:
Raincoast, 9050 Shaughnessy St, Vancouver, BC V6P 6E5.
Tel.: (1) 604 323 7100; Fax: (1) 604 323 2600

A catalogue record for this book is available from the British Library.

ISBN: 978-1-84850-635-0

**To Elizabeth,
for so many deep conversations
about the nature of reality**

'You speak of destiny as if it was fixed.'
Phillip Pullman, *The Golden Compass*

CONTENTS

ACKNOWLEDGEMENTS

I am deeply grateful to my partner, Elizabeth Caproni, for helping me so much with this book. We had many long philosophical conversations about destiny, free will, the nature of reality, consciousness, and God. After the first few I decided to record them using the memo feature on my iPhone. Playing them back was a wonderful reminder of our conversations and of how deeply we delved into the subjects. They eventually formed the basis of numerous aspects of the book. Without those conversations (and wine!), this book might have had far fewer pages.

I'm also grateful to the audiences who gave me some feedback and shared some of their own insights before I started writing and who allowed me to 'test out' the new material. This meant that I was able to write the book more quickly than I ordinarily would because so much of the material, and my ways of describing difficult concepts, were fresh in my mind. I'd also like to say thanks to Robert Holden, author of *Shift Happens*, for suggesting I try this out.

I wrote most of this book in Costa Coffee at Windsor Royal Shopping Centre, in Windsor. I am grateful to the staff there for their friendliness and for creating the ideal writing environment for me.

I'd also like to express my deep gratitude to my editor, Lizzie Hutchins, for doing such a wonderful job in editing this book, especially given the very tight timescale she had.

And I am grateful to Jo Burgess and Michelle Pilley at Hay House in London for giving me so much guidance throughout my development as an author, and also to Julie Oughton for allowing me to stretch my original deadline for this book and so compress all of the publishing timelines – again!

INTRODUCTION

Is your life mapped out? I'm tempted to give you my answer in a single word, but things aren't quite as clear-cut as 'yes' or 'no.' You'll see why as you read on. But, just to give you a bit of a teaser, the answer is kind of 'yes,' 'no,' and 'yes and no.' Confused?

Probably not nearly as much as I was when I first found the scientific research that suggests that we change the *past* from the present. It was a real curve ball. I had figured that a sense of the *future* might influence choices in the present, but I hadn't really considered that the present might influence choices in the past. That throws a bit of a spanner in the works, just when you think you have everything pretty much figured out!

I've been figuring some of these subjects out for nearly three decades, and I'm only 41 at the moment. It has surprised me that many of my conclusions haven't really changed that much since I was a child. Maybe I was running on pure intuition then, but what I have done since is search for scientific evidence that can both confirm and explain my ideas.

In the early chapters of this book you'll learn about some of what I call the 'forces of destiny' – the forces that act upon us all. Some are internal and some are external. You'll learn about chronobiology, for example, which describes how solar and lunar cycles drive our biological rhythms, from when (and why) we go to sleep to how we react to sunlight. Since these cycles run like clockwork, and will do so well past our lifetimes, part of our biological destiny is written in the cosmos.

You'll also learn about genetics as a force of destiny. We are born with a share of the genes of each of our parents, and so some of our traits are mapped out before we are even able to speak. But the science of epigenetics shows us that we can overrule our genes much of the time.

You'll also read about presentiment and the numerous research studies that show how our nervous system reacts to the future before the future occurs. I've also discussed mind–matter interactions and what they mean for us.

The subject of destiny inevitably led me into writing about the nature of reality, consciousness, and God. I really love these subjects. I'm aware that the ideas I present might not appeal to everyone, but I have enjoyed writing about them all the same.

There are some practical suggestions too: I've summarized key points at the end of each chapter and have also listed a few 'life experiments' that can guide you toward a deeper, richer understanding of the concepts.

Quite apart from any debate over destiny and free will, there is no question that our actions have effects, and therefore we create much of what we experience in life. It works in three ways and I call these the 'three levels of creation.' I won't give too much more away at the moment – I'll leave you to read about them later.

I've also included a set of 'Ten Spiritual and Practical Secrets for Attracting What You Want.' I'll leave you to read about them too, but let's just say that they are the wisest things I've ever learned, and they present a map for getting from where you are now to where you want to be.

A few of my readers might recognize some of the topics in this book from a book I wrote back in 2007 called *Destiny vs Free Will*. At first I set out to update the book with new ideas, but eventually I just wrote a whole new book. In the process I borrowed a small number of concepts from that initial book and re-wrote and updated them, but I also added much, much more new scientific research and ideas so that the two books are now very different.

As odd as it might sound, I'm really going to miss writing this book. Immersing myself in the question of whether our life is mapped out has been immensely satisfying and rewarding for me. I hope you enjoy reading the book too. If you enjoy it half as much as I enjoyed writing it then you'll sense that I'm smiling right now.

CHAPTER 1

CHRONOBIOLOGY

'Our great symbol for the Goddess is the moon, whose three aspects reflect the three stages in women's lives and whose cycles of waxing and waning coincide with women's menstrual cycles.'

CAROL P. CHRIST

There was once a ship's captain named Androsthenes, who was serving under Alexander the Great in the fourth century BC when he noted that leaf movements on a tamarind tree followed the sun. That was the first known description of a circadian rhythm.[1]

In 1729, Jean-Jacques d'Ortous de Mairan, a French scientist who was studying the movements of plant leaves, also noted their rhythm, but, importantly, he noted that it even occurred when the plants were held in darkness. This prompted the idea that there might be an internal (known as endogenous) process that responded to external (in this case solar) sources.

Circadian rhythms can be very precise. Some flowers actually open with such precision that Carolus Linnaeus, a Swedish botanist and naturalist, even created a 'floral clock' in 1751.[2] He set out different plants in a circle, all of which flowered at a certain time. For instance, the hawk's beard plant would open its flowers at 5 a.m. and an hour later, at 6 a.m., the hawkweed would open its flowers, and the white water lily would follow at 7 a.m. As time passed throughout the day, the floral clock would accurately tell the time.

Chronobiology is the science that studies how living organisms adapt to the rhythms of the sun and the moon to produce biological rhythms. The name itself comes from the Greek word *chronos*, which means 'time,' giving us chronobiology, or 'time'-biology.

Chronobiological rhythms are very important to us. Most obviously, they affect our sleeping and waking cycles, but many of our other biological rhythms are tuned to solar and lunar cycles, including eating, hormone production, and even cellular regeneration. In animals, hibernation and mating are also chronobiological rhythms – seasonal ones.

We often talk about these commonplace things without ever giving a thought to the fact that these biological rhythms owe their existence to the movements of the Earth, sun, and moon. It's the Earth's rotation that produces the effect of the sun moving across the sky, for instance. It's not the sun that moves: the Earth is spinning.

I remember mentioning biological rhythms being tuned to cosmic cycles to a scientist colleague, whose response was that it 'reeked of astrology' and was 'obviously pseudoscience, mate!' He even scoffed at chronobiology as an 'obviously made-up word.' Yet, as I pointed out to him, every high-school biology student is aware of the process of photosynthesis and that it owes its existence to the sun's rays, which are periodic – a consequence of the spinning of the Earth on its axis. Why does grass grow in the summer but not in the winter? Because there's more sunlight in the summer and it's warmer then. And why is that? It's to do with the rotation of the Earth around the sun.

Chronobiology is important because it shows us that our biology is affected by cosmic cycles.[3] And since cosmic cycles are so precise – we can predict the movements of the Earth, sun, and moon with startling accuracy for thousands of years – we can think of them as forces of destiny in that we can therefore predict future biological changes that will occur in our body as a result of them. In that sense, some aspects of our life *are* mapped out.

There are many chronobiological rhythms. The most important ones for us are circadian rhythms. These are typically 24-hour cycles, although there are well-known longer and shorter ones. For instance, the menstrual cycle is known as an *infradian* rhythm, which is a cycle whose period is longer than a day.[4] The approximate duration of this cycle is linked with the 'period' of rotation of the moon around the Earth. In animals, reproductive cycles and annual migration patterns are also examples of infradian rhythms.

Cycles shorter than 24 hours are known as *ultradian* rhythms. A typical example is the sleep cycle that includes REM (rapid eye movement), which is the time we are dreaming. It is about 90 minutes long. There's also a three-hour cycle of growth hormone production and even a two-and-a-half to four-hour nasal cycle. This is a rhythmic congestion and then decongestion cycle of the nasal cavities. It is governed by the autonomic nervous system (ANS), which tells us that a cosmic cycle (the rotation of the Earth) affects the human nervous system.

We are typically a *diurnal* species, meaning we are most active during daylight hours, although some people are a little more *nocturnal*. These differences are called *chronotypes*. I am definitely a 'morning person' because I feel most alert and am at my most productive in the morning. I write mostly in the morning. A *nocturnal* species is more active during the night.

A very important feature of circadian rhythms is that they run deep into the body. They not only have a period of approximately 24 hours, but the 24-hour rhythm continues even under constant conditions – like darkness, for instance. This shows us that the 'clock mechanism' is internal – it is biological in nature. It will run on its own, which tells us that it's been around for a very long time.

Melatonin, the sleep–wake hormone, keeps regular time, rising as the sun goes down and falling as the sun comes up. Its effects cause sleepiness and wakefulness.[5] Even when we go to a different place in the world, where the sun is in a different part of the sky, the rhythm remains constant according to our previous location before gradually synchronizing with the new location. That is the second very important feature we need to consider: entrainment! This is where the clock synchronizes with our movements.

Both the clock mechanism and entrainment are responsible for the feeling of jet-lag. If we get on a plane mid-afternoon and fly for, say, ten hours in a westward direction so that we arrive at 2 p.m. local time, even though the sun is shining when we land, our body clock thinks it's midnight because melatonin levels are still in their home rhythm. So we feel tired. But then our melatonin rhythm gradually synchronizes with the melatonin rhythm set by the sun's position in our new location: it *entrains* to the new time zone and we start to feel more alert in the evenings.

This demonstrates the synchronization of human biology with the sun – with the rotation of the Earth on its axis.

We also get oscillations in vitamin D levels in our body according to the intensity of sunlight. Here's something that we don't tend to think about, but as vitamin D deficiency is linked with some diseases (childhood rickets and possibly multiple sclerosis), we can actually say that these diseases are in some way causally linked with the movements of the Earth and sun in space. Our biology is tuned to the heavens. We can't disentangle ourselves from nature's cycles.

While we're on the subject of vitamin D, it has been reported that skin cancer awareness has turned people away from the sun, but at the other end of the scale it has led to an increase in rickets, which is caused by a vitamin D deficiency.

As well as chemical oscillations, there are also genetic oscillations in our biology in response to the sun. This is where a number of genes are activated more or less often during daylight hours. Here, we see that we are synched with heavenly movements right down to the genetic level.

GENETIC CLOCKS

Yes, we have a genetic clock! Its first component – the 'period' gene – was discovered in the early 1970s in the fruit fly, *Drosophila melanogaster*.[6] That gene plays a central role in driving the chemistry of the circadian rhythm. But it wasn't until 1994 that the first example was discovered in humans. Now known as the 'CLOCK' (Circadian Locomotor Output Cycles Kaput) gene, it was discovered by Joseph Takahashi.[7]

The CLOCK gene affects the period of circadian rhythms. When it is active, it produces proteins that switch on biological pathways that run our circadian rhythms. It is the first domino of a biochemical domino effect.

Our internal 'master clock' is in the hypothalamus of the brain, in a pair of cells found in a region known as the suprachiasmatic nucleus (SCN).[8] Photosensitive cells (ones that are sensitive to sunlight) in the retina of the eye detect levels of sunlight and then communicate this information to the cells in the SCN. The SCN then passes the information to the pineal gland, which secretes melatonin.

There are other clocks in the body too. They are known as 'peripheral clocks' and can be found in the liver, lungs, spleen, pancreas, thymus, oesophagus, and skin. Like all genes, there are variations of them, known as polymorphs. It is the polymorphs of the CLOCK gene that have been linked with insomnia, difficulty losing weight, diurnal preference, mood disorders, and also the recurrence of major depressive episodes in patients with bipolar disorder, further cementing the idea that our body is genetically tuned to some cosmic cycles.

This fact – that gene activity is linked with cosmic activity – is quite humbling. It tells us very clearly that we are not separate from nature, nor from her cycles. Where nature goes, we go too. We are bound to her destiny and thus some of life is mapped out for us.

We are in fact so dependent upon the circadian rhythm that there are health problems associated with disruption of the rhythm – for example, seasonal affective disorder (SAD) and delayed sleep phase syndrome.

In 2010 researchers at the Lighting Research Center at the Rensselaer Polytechnic Institute in New York found that when eighth-grade students had lighting disrupted in the morning for five days during the school week it impacted the onset of their sleep, so that they experienced disruption in sleeping patterns, which in turn could negatively affect performance and alertness.[9]

It has even been reported that bipolar disorder patients with a circadian rhythm disturbance are helped through the effect of lithium (an antidepressant) on the CLOCK gene.

THE EVOLUTION OF THE HUMAN CLOCK

The predestined rhythm of day, night, day, night, day, etc, is like a heartbeat driving biological evolution. We have evolved to have circadian rhythms – to be in synch with the heavenly dance. Not only do our eyes and our skin respond to sunlight, but it is believed that circadian rhythms actually evolved as a protection mechanism, shielding early cells from the sun's UV radiation and causing replication to occur in the dark when there was less chance of UV-induced mutations.

Most people are completely unaware that we have evolved within cosmic cycles. But we have circadian rhythms because biological life evolved within the periodic peaks and troughs in temperature and sunlight. This is *why* the 'period' and CLOCK genes exist today: biology adapted to the cosmic cycles.

Some of the body's rhythms were 'set' not only to sunlight but to the seasonal availability of food – plant life and animal meat (some animals hibernate in the winter) – all of which created a chemical environment in the body within which the human genome evolved.

The central fact that the *rhythm remains under constant conditions* is because it has been tuned to cosmic movements over eons of biological evolution.

So the cosmos exerts a force of destiny upon us whether we like it or not, or whether we agree with it or not. We are a part of heavenly cycles.

LUNAR CYCLES

As well as being influenced by the movement of the Earth and sun, we are also influenced by that of the moon. Not only does its gravity drag billions of tons of water over the surface of the planet twice a day to create the tides, but the average time of women's menstrual cycles is approximately the same as the period of time it takes the moon to travel around the Earth.

In one scientific study of 826 women, 28 percent were found to begin menstruating during the four days around the new moon – the phase where the moon is at its smallest and is beginning a new cycle, but no more than 13 percent began menstruating during any other four-day period of the month.[10] In other words, twice as many women begin menstruation around a new moon than at any other time in the month.

Another study, published in the *Journal of Obstetrics and Gynaecology*, found that the onset of labor peaked at 8 p.m. and 9 a.m., which is related to hormonal rhythms and therefore may be linked to solar or lunar positions.[11]

The lunar correlation extends beyond human biology, which of course it should do, as all biology has evolved within the same heavenly cycles. Dr. Frank Brown of Northwestern University, USA, found a correlation between the moon and the opening of oysters.[12] He shifted a group of oysters 1,600km (1,000 miles) inland, from Long Island Sound to Evanston, Illinois, and studied them. In darkened and pressurized tanks, the oysters continued to open and close their valves to the rhythms of the tides at Long Island. But after about two weeks, they began to change. Their opening and closing rhythms began to synchronize with what they would be if there were tides in Evanston – in effect, they began to synchronize with the movement of the moon, just as our melatonin rhythm gradually synchronizes with current conditions when we travel across the world.

When I was a child, the cosmos fascinated me. Some of the earliest trivia I knew was trivia about the planets – how long they took to rotate around the sun, how many moons they had, and so on. Even now, one of my favorite books is called *Universe*. It is a big color book of the planets, stars, galaxies, nebulas, and many other cosmic phenomena. There are few things I find more relaxing than looking up at the stars on a clear night.

When I got my first telescope, I spent countless hours studying the moon. At the time I was completely ignorant of its effects upon me. The moon has been the subject of much folklore – and there might be more to this than just moonshine.

A study published in the *Medical Journal of Australia* examined hospital admissions for self-poisoning around the time of a full moon, which is 14 days after a new moon and when the moon is at its largest.[13] Looking at 2,215 admissions between 1988 and 1993, the researchers found that women were more likely to overdose than men at the time of a new moon, but that men were more likely to overdose than women at the time of a full moon. Specifically, they found that women were 15 percent less likely to take an overdose around the time of a full moon than they were around the time of a new moon and even suggested that a full moon was protective for women.

People have talked about the moon's ability to affect human behavior for centuries. The werewolf myth derives from this – representing madness caused by a full moon. A number of mental health workers have actually noted that the more disturbed a patient is, the greater the moon's effect on them. In 1842 the Lunacy Act in the UK actually defined a lunatic as someone who was 'rational during the first two phases of the moon and afflicted with a period of fatuity in the period following the full moon.' It might be that the moon can exert more measurable effects on people who are emotionally vulnerable or disturbed.

******

So, the fact that our biology is so entangled with the movements of the Earth, sun, and moon tells us that life isn't quite a totally blank canvas that we can paint as we wish. It *is* mapped out for us in some respects.

In the next chapter, we'll explore some more cosmic cycles and the ways in which they affect us too.

KEY POINTS

- Our biology is tuned to solar and lunar cycles. This is called chronobiology.

- The CLOCK gene sets off our internal chronobiology.

- The most important rhythms for us are circadian rhythms.

- Cosmic cycles can be thought of as forces of destiny.

LIFE EXPERIMENTS

• Next time you travel to a different time zone, remind yourself that jet-lag is because your melatonin rhythm is still tuned to your previous location.

• Watch how your houseplants or plants in your garden point themselves toward the sun. Reflect on the fact that this is because the rotation of the Earth is causing the sun to move in the sky and this is impacting the plants' biology.

CHAPTER 2

WRITTEN IN THE STARS

'I don't believe in astrology;
I'm a Sagittarius and we're skeptical.'

ARTHUR C. CLARKE

So, we know that cycles of the Earth, sun, and moon act like a force of destiny upon our biology. We have learned about the effects of sunlight, which pulses for each of us with the rotation of the Earth in space, but the sun is also responsible for impacting us in more subtle, but also important ways.

THE SOUND OF THE SUN

The sun is a massive ball of hot gas. It is so hot that it heats us up even though we are 150 million km (93 million miles) away from it. It provides us with heat and light – that much we know – but there is other activity on the sun that affects us too.

Solar activity rises and falls through a cycle of approximately 11 years, which is known as the solar cycle or sunspot cycle.[1] At the peaks, there are more sunspots, and there are also more frequent ejections of energy from the sun, known as coronal mass ejections (CMEs), where the sun spits out billions of tons of charged particles.

Solar cycle 24 is due to peak early in 2013, give or take a few months, and solar cycle 25 is scheduled to peak around 2023/2024. What does it mean for us?

When the charged particles from a coronal mass ejection reach us, we see the northern lights (aurora borealis). They interact with and bounce off part of our planetary magnetic field (the geomagnetic field), rippling across the sky like rain on a tin roof.

Another name for the northern lights is a 'geomagnetic storm.' This storm is just like a weather storm except it's the geomagnetic field that's turbulent.[2] Geomagnetic storms are a major component of what's called 'space weather.' They can be pretty severe – so violent in fact that they can knock out satellites and sensitive electronic equipment.

On March 13, 1989, for instance (around the peak of solar cycle 22), a geomagnetic storm knocked out Canada's Hydro-Quebec power grid in just a couple of seconds, leaving six million people with no electricity for nine hours. People as far south as Texas were able to see the corresponding northern lights, which is testimony to the storm's strength, as usually only very northern or southern regions, near the poles, can see the light show.

On July 14, 2000 (around the peak of solar cycle 23), a coronal mass ejection erupted in what is known as the Bastille Day Event. Fortunately for us, it didn't cause any damage. But between

October 29 and November 2, 2003 (still associated with solar cycle 23), a series of 17 major solar flares, in what is now referred to as the 'Halloween storm,' were so strong that the Japanese ADEOS-2 satellite was severely damaged and operational problems occurred in many other satellites.

The most severe geomagnetic storm ever recorded lasted from August 28 to September 2, 1859. It produced a solar 'superstorm' that is known today as the Carrington Event. It was so severe that many telegraph operators across the northern hemisphere received shocks. People in Hawaii, Mexico, Cuba, and even Italy could see the northern lights.

A modern-day Carrington Event would knock out power grids and radio communications all around the world, disrupt GPS devices, seriously disrupt airplane navigation systems, disrupt the internet, and cause billions of dollars' worth of damage to satellites. In fact, very recently, a coronal mass ejection from a distant star ripped the atmosphere right off a planet (exoplanet HD189733b) close to it.

You can keep up to date with magnetic storms through NASA's 'Space Weather' website if you're interested.[3] I get regular e-mails alerting me to when one is on its way. They're fairly numerous at the moment (2012).

GEOMAGNETIC STORMS AND BIOLOGY

Each time there's a geomagnetic storm, there are changes in the Earth's geomagnetic field.

It's really handy that the Earth has a geomagnetic field, actually, because the charged particles emanating from a CME can cause chromosome damage and cancer. If an astronaut had been walking on the moon during the Carrington Event, it would have been fatal, because the moon doesn't have a geomagnetic field and a large dose of the radiation is pretty much lethal.

The Earth's geomagnetic field fluctuates not just on account of geomagnetic storms, but also owing to changes in the solar wind (a constant stream of particles from the sun) and even the movements of the moon.

What's relevant to the main topic of this book is the growing body of scientific evidence that shows that changes in the Earth's geomagnetic field affect biology and behavior, both human and animal. And since geomagnetic storms are roughly predictable, we can view these, too, as forces of destiny.

Some people doubt that we can be sensitive to the Earth's geomagnetic field, given that its strength is fairly weak, but it is likely that we have become attuned to it over evolutionary timescales. Indeed, the body of evidence for its effect on biology is now so strong that it contributed to the International Union of Radio Science establishing Commission K, whose purpose is to study the effects of electromagnetics on biology and medicine.

Recent studies have shown, for instance, that homing pigeons, whales, and dolphins can get lost during geomagnetic storms because they have a magnetically sensitive mineral called magnetite in bundles of their nerve fibers.[4] This allows them to use the Earth's geomagnetic field to navigate.

It has even been suggested that increased solar activity might contribute to bees getting lost. It is well known that they use the Earth's geomagnetic field as one of several navigation cues. They communicate the location of nectar by using a series of elaborate movements, but they might make mistakes during geomagnetic storms, sending members of their hive off in the wrong direction.

Similarly, when University of Cambridge scientist Margaret Klinowska plotted the positions of mass strandings of whales onto a map that showed the contours of the Earth's geomagnetic field (which looks a bit like a contour map of hills and valleys), she discovered that most strandings around England occurred where magnetic 'valleys' went from the water to the shore.[5]

In May 2004, scientists at Virginia Tech, publishing their results in the prestigious journal *Nature*, suggested that some birds could actually see the lines of the Earth's magnetic field.[6] They proposed that the birds saw patterns of color or light intensity superimposed upon their visual surroundings, and that this was due to certain types of chemicals (known as photoreceptors and photopigments) present in the retina that were sensitive to magnetic fields.

In a practical demonstration of using the geomagnetic field for direction-finding, scientists at Tel Aviv University studied blind mole rats who clearly couldn't navigate using visual cues.[7] One group of rats was placed in a maze and the scientists watched as they moved to the southern sector to set up home. Then the scientists flipped the magnetic field round so that it pointed the opposite way. This time the mole rats set up home in the northern sector. They were using the magnetic field to navigate their way home.

We see the same kind of geomagnetic field-assisted navigation with monarch butterflies. In autumn each year, the monarch butterfly flutters over 3,200km (2,000 miles) from the USA and Canada to the warmer climate of Mexico. It was always a mystery how these butterflies, and indeed almost all birds that migrate to warmer climates, could make such very long journeys to exactly the same place every year without getting lost. Many birds fly thousands of miles to another continent, and when they return they will end up not only in the area they set off from months earlier, but in the same garden on the same branch of the same tree.

So, in 1999, scientists at the University of Kansas placed some monarch butterflies in a tabletop arena. They noted that when they flew it was in a southwesterly direction, as if they were flying from the USA or Canada to Mexico. Then they shielded the arena from the Earth's geomagnetic field. This time the butterflies fluttered in random directions, indicating that they had been using the geomagnetic field to head southwest.[8]

In a similar US experiment, scientists at the University of North Carolina at Chapel Hill studied young loggerhead turtles.[9] Just as birds fly thousands of miles and end up back on the same tree, so these turtles swim thousands of miles and end up back on the tiny strip of beach they were born on. They typically migrate along the North Atlantic gyre, from the east coast of the USA across the Atlantic Ocean, down the coast of Spain, down the coast of Africa and then back across the ocean and up to the

USA in a clockwise circle. So the scientists filled a container with saltwater to simulate the ocean. Then they placed wires around the container to produce a magnetic field similar to the Earth's geomagnetic field. When the turtles were placed in the container they swam in a circular motion, as if they were following the gyre.

THE GEOMAGNETIC FIELD AND HUMANS

In many ways, our genome is similar to the genomes of animals. Clearly we mostly use visual cues to get around, but it is likely that we have a latent ability to use the Earth's geomagnetic field too. It's known as magnetoreception.

In an attempt to test it, Dr. Robin Baker of Manchester University in the UK blindfolded some students and drove them up to 48km (30 miles) away from the university. Then he asked them to estimate the direction of the university. They scored pretty well. But when he removed their blindfolds, they became disoriented.

He then did a similar experiment with groups of schoolchildren. One group had bar magnets attached to their heads that would swamp out the Earth's geomagnetic field, and the other group had magnetized pieces of metal attached to their heads. When they were asked to indicate north, the children who had the magnetized pieces of metal on their heads performed much better than the group with the magnets on.[10]

While he was head of the Neuroscience Laboratory at Laurentian University in Ontario, Canada, neuroscientist Michael Persinger also showed that the human brain was sensitive to magnetic fields. In several studies he was able to induce mystical experiences in people by applying a magnetic field to the temporal lobes of the brain.[11]

He also proposed that wobbles of the Earth's geomagnetic field (which can be caused by solar or lunar activity) could also bring about this effect.

Other research, at the University of St. Petersburg in Russia, has shown that geomagnetic storms can affect EEG patterns in the brain, particularly in the frontal and central areas of the brain.[12]

Some research has even found links between geomagnetic storms and depression. For example, Dr. Ronald Kay, a consultant psychiatrist at the Westbank Clinic in Falkirk, Scotland (close to where I was born), studied the records of patients admitted to the Lothian Hospital in Scotland for depression between 1976 and 1986 and compared them with records of geomagnetic storms.[13] He found a stunning correlation. When he looked at hospital admissions during the first, second, and third week after a geomagnetic storm he found that there was a 9 percent increase in male admissions for depressed-phase manic-depressive illness (bipolar disorder) in the first week, a 36 percent increase in the second week, and an 8 percent increase after the third; there were no relationships in periods when there had been no magnetic storms.

In 2006, Michael Berk, a psychiatry professor at Australia's University of Melbourne, also found a correlation between geomagnetic storms and mental health.[14] While examining the suicide statistics for Australia between 1968 and 2002 (68,172 suicides; 51,845 men and 16,327 women), and comparing them with the time of geomagnetic storms, he found that suicides increased significantly in women during concurrent periods of geomagnetic storms.

Both these pieces of research are suggestive of the sensitivity of vulnerable people to geomagnetic activity. And since that activity is part of a cosmic cycle, it represents an important force of destiny for some people.

The increase in depression has been linked with melatonin levels, which also have a role in chronobiology. Unsurprisingly, some researchers have discovered that geomagnetic storms can impact the melatonin rhythm, which is suggestive of an effect on the CLOCK gene.

The effects of magnetic storms have even found their way into the world of finance. In a study conducted by the Federal Reserve Bank of Atlanta in 2003, it was found that in the week after high geomagnetic storm activity there was a downturn on stock returns.[15]

Can we say that the financial crises that began in 2008 are totally independent of solar (or other cosmic) activity? I'm not so sure we can, even if it sounds unlikely, especially as they were a result of human activity and we are not exactly independent of nature's cycles. The actual association is probably complex and subtle, but solar activity does affect some human biology and behavior.

GEOMAGNETIC STORMS AND THE HEART

Geomagnetic storms have also been shown to affect the heart and blood pressure.[16] Research has shown that blood pressure increases along with geomagnetic storm intensity.

In 2001 a team of scientists also found that the erythrocyte sedimentation rate (ESR) of ischaemic heart patients was significantly altered during a geomagnetic storm. The ESR rate is the speed at which red blood cells fall to the bottom of a test tube. When there is inflammation, blood proteins clump together and make the blood 'heavier,' and so the cells fall to the bottom more quickly. So the research was indicative of increased inflammation, which is an indicator of stress in the cardiovascular system, on account of geomagnetic storm activity. Fortunately, the scientists found that they could easily protect patients with high sensitivity from the storms by creating a shielding chamber.

Concerned about the possible angina-causing effects of geomagnetic storms, other scientists tested the anti-inflammatory effects of aspirin and found that it decreased the negative effects of the storms because it counteracted inflammation and so thinned the blood.

EXTRA-SENSITIVE PERCEPTION

As the body of research showing how we're affected by geomagnetic storms is increasing, it has become clear that some people are more sensitive than others, which isn't surprising.

Researchers have labelled the sensitive people 'aurora disturbance sensitive people' (ADSP).[17] For these people, the effect of a geomagnetic storm might not be unlike the effect of caffeine in coffee, inclining them toward stress or agitation.

The work on geomagnetic storms has also shone a little light upon the phenomenon of geopathic stress. The term derives from the Greek for 'disease of the Earth' and refers to how sensitive people fall ill in certain geographical regions. Some people are believed to fall ill in certain buildings. It is actually considered the norm in some European countries to have a geopathic stress survey done before buying a property.

The reason for geopathic stress in certain regions might be that the Earth's geomagnetic field isn't uniform all over the planet. As mentioned earlier, a geomagnetic contour map resembles a classic contour map showing the heights and depths of hills and valleys. It is most intense at the poles but it is also distorted in many locations by the presence of underground rock formations, mineral concentrations, volcanic activity, and underground water.

If a person is sensitive to changes in the Earth's geomagnetic field, or at least some systems of the body pick it out from the background of technologically created fields, then highs or lows in the field might be responsible for them feeling a little off-color in some places.

Changes in the geomagnetic field don't always produce negative effects, of course. It is just that these have been the most studied.

For most people there will be few or no observable effects. But, given that we have evolved within the background of cosmic solar activity, it would be understandable if some people were found to be more sensitive, perhaps having some genetic polymorphism that could increase their sensitivity.

For some people solar activity might even produce mystical and enlightening experiences. As noted earlier, Michael Persinger found that some people had mystical experiences when he stimulated their brain with magnetic fields similar to the Earth's during a geomagnetic storm. Perhaps mystical experiences are 'written in the stars' for some people, just as depression or high blood pressure could be written for others, dependent on each person's unique biology, or even chronotype.

******

Whatever the case may be, there is no question that cosmic cycles affect us. And they are regular and therefore predictable, so it's no surprise that events in life tend to be cyclic too. Have you ever noticed that some events in your life have repeated themselves? It's the same in the world at large, where we see political swings back and forth, cyclic fashion trends, and even the rise and fall of civilizations. In my opinion this phenomenon is in some way linked to the cyclic nature of the cosmos in that we are 'programmed' to do things cyclically.

So, life might be mapped out to an extent. Rather than being completely independent of, and masters of, nature, we are in fact led by nature, even though we don't notice this most of the time.

I like the metaphor of a small rowing boat on a wide river. We can think of free will as using our oars to paddle to where we want to go, but there is a cosmic current on the metaphorical river. We tend to pay it no heed because we seem to have the freedom to choose where we want to go. But, regardless of our choices, we do follow the current.

In the next chapter, we shall add yet another current to our metaphoric river – the genetic one.

KEY POINTS

- Solar magnetic activity is periodic, reaching a peak every 11 years.

- The periodic pulse of geomagnetic storms affects satellites, power grids, and human biology.

- Some animals use the Earth's geomagnetic field for navigation.

- We also recognize the geomagnetic field and may have a latent ability to use it for orienting ourselves.

- Geomagnetic field changes can affect the brain and the heart, both as a consequence of geomagnetic storms and due to changes in the contours of the geomagnetic field.

LIFE EXPERIMENTS

- Which aspects of your life have repeated in the past or are repeating now – both good and bad?

- Awareness of these patterns gives us an opportunity to make changes so that we don't repeat any errors or painful episodes. With an awareness of your own cycles, what decisions can you make now to set your life on a new trajectory?

- What aspects of global life seem to be repeating the cycles of the past?

CHAPTER 3

WRITTEN IN OUR GENES

'Scientists have found the gene for shyness. They would have found it years ago, but it was hiding behind a couple of other genes.'

JONATHAN KATZ

Now that we know how cosmic movements affect our life, it's time to turn our attention to more internal forces: our genes.

The force of genes is quite obvious really. If your parents are tall then there is a fair chance that you'll be tall as well. So, rather than your biology at birth being a blank canvas, it is filled in by the biology of your parents. The same can be said for emotional traits and artistic leanings, too.

Most people do actually assume that genes are a form of destiny, even though we tend not to use that word when we talk of genetics. Most of us think of destiny as the flow of events of our life. We also generally accept that having a 'tall person gene' will make us tall. But there's a new take on the seemingly destined role of genetics.

EPIGENETICS

A science known as epigenetics has started to examine the influence of the environment and personal choices on the actual *behavior* of genes, and therefore genetic 'destiny.' How a gene behaves is far more important than whether we have a gene or not.

Research has shown that free will can, to an extent, overrule genetics. For example, certain choices in how you lead your life can impact the likelihood of you ever developing heart problems, even if you are part of a family with a long history of heart problems and have genes that increase your likelihood of the disease.

So, rather than it being nature (genes) *or* nurture (the environment), according to the popular debate that's gone on for years, the general consensus now is that it's actually a bit of both. It's nature *and* nurture. It's destiny *and* free will.

To what extent then do genes influence what happens in life? Well, let's take height. Most people assume that height is totally genetic. Actually, it's not. It's about 80 percent genetic, or 'heritable,' to use the technically correct term, This roughly means that 80 percent of the average person's height is a product of their genes, and 20 percent is a product of their influences in life.

We know this from genetic studies on identical twins who were separated at birth and brought up in different families. They grow up to be the same height about 80 percent of the time (on average). The disparity is down to their diet, lifestyle, early influences, and even parenting. A well-loved baby, for instance, receiving lots of care and attention in an emotionally rich environment, will tend to grow larger than a baby who is deprived of love and human connection, even when they have identical genes.

Love and human contact actually make sure that the genes that produce human growth hormone (HGH) and the hormone oxytocin are activated as much as they need to be for normal growth.[1] When love and contact are relatively absent, the genes are less active. So, life experiences very much sway the activity of the genes.

Let's look at another example. Some people believe that happiness is all in the genes, others that it's all in the mind. You've probably guessed by now that I'm going to say it's a bit of both. Great. You get it!

Studies show that happiness is about 50 percent in the genes. The rest is down to life experiences, personal improvement strategies (self-help work), and even how your friends are feeling. In fact, research at Harvard University in the USA found that approximately 25 percent of the average person's happiness was a consequence of the emotional state of their friends.[2]

And the 50-percent-in-the-genes stat is actually just an average over a number of people. For some people the genetics of happiness are stronger, causing them to be, well, just plain happy most of the time (gits!). For others, happiness is really mostly down to their own choices and experiences. They have to work at it. And I would guess that, even if a person's genes destined them to be less than happy, chances are their personal choices and experiences in life could make all the difference.

So, we inherit genes from our parents, who got theirs from their parents, which means that we have 25 percent of each of our grandparents' genes, and therefore 12.5 percent of each of our great-grandparents' genes. I'm one-sixteenth Spanish on my dad's side, meaning that I got 6.25 percent of my genes from my dad's Spanish great-grandmother.

Where am I going with this? Well, you can see that part of your height and your happiness, as well as loads of other things, are linked with the heights and emotional states of your ancestors, so there's a seeming force of destiny there. When you were born you were immediately pushed out into genetic currents of destiny. But your choices and life experiences provide you with a paddle that will often be such a good paddle that you can paddle right out of a current you don't want to be in.

Where the subject gets even more interesting, I think, is that the actual life experiences of your parents and grandparents affect your genes too. This is where the science of epigenetics reaches new heights.

Incredibly, we now know that stuff that happens to our parents and grandparents affects them at the genetic level, and they can pass the effect on to us. So, we not only inherit their genes, but also a bit of what happened to them in their lives.

We can think of their experiences as leaving a little mark on their genes, like an emblem, that gets passed down the generations, just as we might pass on a family heirloom. The emblem affects how some of their genes behave and therefore how some of our genes behave too.

The experiences of our parents and grandparents don't actually change their DNA sequence, in case you were wondering. That remains intact. But the emblem alters the way that the genetic code is read. It's like the director of a film making notes on a script so that the actor interprets it in a different way from how it was written, and then subsequent actors also playing the role according to the director's notes as well, rather than following the script.

So, as surprising as it might sound, some of the experiences in your parents' and grandparents' lives can set the tone for your life, acting like a force of destiny even though you might be completely unaware of what they got up to.

YOU ARE WHAT YOUR GRANDPARENTS ATE

The term 'you are what you eat' is very true in my opinion. I like to have a healthy diet because I find that my body and mind work better when I do. It's a play on words, though. I'm not exactly a stick of broccoli, although I'll bet you don't know that we share about 60 percent of our genetic code with broccoli (and cabbage and cauliflower). Weird, isn't it?

What I mean by the term 'you are what your grandparents ate' is that their diets can leave an epigenetic emblem on their genes that can be passed on to their kids (your parents), and they in turn can pass it on to you. It's a game of genetic 'pass the parcel.'

This became quite clear from studies on the survivors of the Dutch famine of 1944–5. There was a Nazi food and fuel blockade during the Second World War, and over 30,000 people died of starvation in Holland between 1944 and 1945 as a consequence. Those who survived passed the legacy of their hunger to succeeding generations, impacting their children and their children's children – on and on like a ripple effect through time.[3]

In particular, if the famine hit when a pregnant woman was in her third trimester, she was likely to give birth to a baby whose birth weight was lower than average. And then the baby grew up to be smaller than average throughout their entire life. This current of destiny was set by the malnourishment of the mother during her pregnancy.

On the other hand, if the mother experienced the famine only during her first trimester (so the baby was conceived late in the period of the famine), and ate normally for the remainder of her pregnancy, she was likely to give birth to a baby whose birth weight was normal. In effect, the fetus caught up when the mother was better fed. But that's not the end of the story. Even though the baby's weight caught up, the programming that occurred during the first trimester affected the growing child all the way into adulthood. When these babies grew into adults they had higher obesity rates than the national population.

You might wonder how this happened, considering that these babies were born with seemingly normal weights. It is to do with the environment in the womb during pregnancy. The theory goes that the cells of a growing fetus slow down their metabolism in the first trimester to compensate for the nutritional deficiencies in their environment. They are, in effect, programmed for life during this first trimester. So, as the child grows into an adult, it retains the slower metabolism and is less able to burn off fat. So a person born to a mother malnourished during her first trimester may have a predisposition toward obesity. Life seems to be mapped out for these people in that area... although you may well guess that I'm about to say that they can overrule it! I'll get to that shortly.

The programming of the genes in the first trimester is known as 'developmental programming,' and it's a hot topic in genetics at the moment. It unambiguously shows us that part of our destiny is down to the experiences of our mothers.

I called this section 'You are what your grandparents ate' because the effect actually continues to the next generation. In the Dutch study, the people whose mothers were malnourished during the first trimester, and who were therefore more likely to be obese, gave birth to babies (the females did at least) whose birth weight was higher than average. So babies born two generations later were experiencing the consequences of part of their grandparents' lives. They were on the same current as their grandmothers.

A similar effect was seen when looking back at records from a remote town called Överkalix, in Sweden, in the late nineteenth and early twentieth centuries.[4] It was a time when there were periods of both food scarcity and food abundance. It turned out that if a man had gone hungry during what is known as his slow growth period (SGP, a normal period of slow growth before puberty, usually between nine and 12 for boys), then his sons had a much lower risk of cardiovascular disease. But if food was abundant during this time and there had been overeating, his grandsons had a four times increased risk of diabetes.

As you would expect, there are many causes of epigenetic modifications during developmental programming. It looks as though drinking alcohol, for instance, which leads to fetal alcohol syndrome, might also lead to epigenetic modifications. Really, any environmental factor, good or bad, will be likely to do so. Studies have suggested that smoking, sustained joy, sustained physical activity, or even a long bout of sexual activity might lead to epigenetic modifications.

Inheriting the effects of our parents' experiences brings to mind the theory of Jean-Baptiste Lamarck, an early nineteenth-century French naturalist who suggested that animals and humans acquired characteristics in life and passed them on to the next generation. His theory has been widely discredited because he suggested that the environment was actually altering the genome, which we know doesn't occur. But, given that nothing was known about the DNA molecule back in Lamarck's time, his theory was actually a fair attempt to explain how we pass on experiences to our children.

In fact, epigenetics does now show us that it is possible to pass on 'acquired characteristics' through epigenetic modifications. Passing our experiences through the generations is known as 'epigenetic inheritance' or 'transgenerational inheritance.'

THE RIPPLE EFFECT

I bet you're wondering how far the ripple effect of epigenetics goes?

It does seem to wear out after a while. The current weakens. Sometimes this is because of the life experiences of the person inheriting the epigenetic modifications.

In 2006 scientists at the Center for Reproductive Biology at Washington State University found that if rat embryos had been exposed to environmental toxins that caused particular diseases, then those diseases (prostate disease, kidney disease, immune system abnormalities, testes abnormalities, and breast cancer development) were passed on for four generations.[5]

Similarly, scientists studying the fruit fly *Drosophila melanogaster* found that when a particular gene called Hsp90 was overactive it produced mutations in the fly (protrusions from its eye) that persisted for a further ten generations.[6]

The effect in humans is unlikely to ripple that far in time. The lifespan of a rodent or fruit fly is considerably shorter than that of humans, so there is less time in one lifespan for life experiences to reprogram the epigenome (the record of epigenetic modifications). But if even part of the effect is representative of genetic behavior in humans then our health today might be influenced by what happened to our great-great-great-grandparents.

So what we do now can affect our children's health, and their children's health, and possibly even that of other generations down the line. Does that make you feel quite responsible? It makes me feel that I want to make some important changes, not only to how I lead my life, but also in the kind of person I am, especially if there's a possibility that my children and grandchildren might benefit. Although I'm not aware of any specific research in the area, I'd hazard a guess that if we made an effort to be more compassionate and kind, then we would influence the likelihood of our children having those traits and in some way would be changing the future world.

We are the guardians of the epigenome of the next generation. Part of our children's destiny is influenced by what we do now, just as part of our own destiny was influenced by what our ancestors did.

The immediate question that arises is: can we deprogram ourselves from epigenetic effects?

STEERING OUT OF AN EPIGENETIC CURRENT

The answer is, broadly, yes, we can.

Going back to the Dutch famine, not all of the people born to late-famine mothers remained small throughout their lives, and not all individuals born to early-famine mothers became obese. It was just a statistically increased risk. So, even though there had been epigenetic modifications, there were two possibilities. Either a) the modifications were randomly different between individuals, so some were programmed to be small, or obese, and some weren't, or b) some people grew up following a particular lifestyle, or in a particular environment, that overruled (or compensated for) the epigenetic modifications.

To be honest, it's likely to have been a bit of both, but what is particularly important for the question we are discussing is that a person's lifestyle and environment can overrule or compensate for the epigenetic modifications during the developmental period. In other words, their choices regarding how they lead their lives can overrule the genetic legacy of their mother's (and father's) life experiences.

So, having 'bad' genes doesn't necessarily confine a person to a life of misery and poor health. Life experiences can actually alter the epigenetic emblems and open up different possibilities. You can think of it as being like the actor deciding that they don't quite agree with the director's notes and scribbling them out, preferring to play the role in their own way.

This suggests that our children aren't necessarily at the mercy of a 'health destiny' laid down by our experiences, or that we are at the mercy of our own ancestry. We can neutralize many of these effects through the lifestyle choices that we make regarding the food we eat, the career or other paths we follow, how we sleep and exercise, and how compassionate we are.

To use an actual lifestyle example regarding nutrition, scientists at Duke University, North Carolina, USA, publishing in *Molecular and Cellular Biology* in 2003, reported that the offspring of mice born with an abnormal gene (agouti gene) that made them yellow and extremely obese were born normal if the mother was given a nutritionally rich diet.[7]

Similarly, in honeybees, it is by being fed royal jelly that one of several genetically identical larvae develops into a queen bee and not a worker.[8]

In a *New York Times* article titled 'Genes as Mirrors of Life Experience,' Thomas Lehner, chief of the genomics research branch of the National Institute of Mental Health, was reported as saying, 'A lot of the model systems we have studied suggest that epigenetic modifications impact behaviour, and also that those effects can be reversed.'[9]

This can shine a light on why some people who have a family history of heart disease or cancer never contract the disease: their lifestyle choices steer them out of a genetic or epigenetic current. It is very clear that having a good diet, taking exercise, and reducing stress levels make all the difference. In light of what we know about epigenetics, it is likely that this lifestyle modifies the epigenome so that a person partly 'predestined' toward heart disease or cancer is no longer at the same risk.

Applying this to physical and mental abilities, it also means that, even if our family hasn't featured anyone good at sports or academically distinguished, we could still become a talented sportsperson or gain a PhD.

A person with 'average intelligence genes' might grow up to be exceptionally intelligent if exposed to the right parents, teachers, and coaches, for instance. The brain of a child is highly 'plastic.' Its growth is easily influenced by its circumstances. A person with 'genius genes,' on the other hand, might not distinguish themselves intellectually if they grow up in an environment which isn't productive for them. Life isn't quite mapped out in the genes. They are just a pencil outline.

IT'S IN THE MIND

Literature and films are full of stories of people who have achieved greatness against all the odds. Others might be born with a genetic edge in terms of size, strength, or other skills, but sheer determination more than compensates in most cases. The 10,000-hour rule (the rule that shows that anyone can become an expert at something after 10,000 hours of committed practice) has shown us that it's really down to what you want and how much you want it. Much of the time, the paddle of free will overrules genetics.

You can see the effects of life experiences even in the way the brain grows. The orbitofrontal cortex (the part behind the orbits of the eyes) grows almost entirely in the 24 months following birth and is extremely responsive to the infant's experiences.[10] A set of loving, responsive parents will ensure that the brain is emotionally nourished and grows well. However, a child with insufficient love and care will likely grow up to have an underdeveloped orbitofrontal cortex. You see this kind of phenomenon in children who have spent that early period of their lives in institutions. So, two genetically identical infants (identical twins) could grow up in different households to have very different brains.

Studies have now shown that enriching life experiences and physical exercise can even promote brain cell growth (neurogenesis) in adults, something that was thought to be impossible only a few years ago.[11] Two genetically identical adults could therefore end up with substantial differences in the same brain regions. The destiny of the brain, so to speak, would take a different trajectory depending on their experiences.

So, when your genes set your boat off on a particular current, if you're prepared to paddle then you can reach a completely different destination. It might take some hard work – especially if you've learned the joys of fast food, or if stress has become a habit – but be encouraged by the knowledge that you really do have the power to overrule your genes.

Quite apart from genetics, the mind itself can overrule the body, showing the power we have to make changes. The placebo effect is a clear demonstration of this. A few years ago, my partner Elizabeth and I were walking in the woods just outside Los Angeles with our friend Olivia. After a while, Olivia realized that we were walking through poison ivy. She immediately panicked. She was terrified that she'd have an allergic reaction. To be honest, embarrassing as it sounds, even though I was in my thirties at the time I didn't know what poison ivy was, so I just shrugged my shoulders and walked on in the firm belief that the little green plants wouldn't cause me any harm. Elizabeth told me she visualized herself protected.

By the next day, Olivia was covered in an itchy rash and Elizabeth and I were fine. That's when I googled poison ivy. Later, when researching the placebo effect for one of my other books, I came across a poison ivy study that made me smile.[12]

In the study, a group of volunteers who were known to be allergic to poison ivy were blindfolded and had their arms rubbed with a leaf. They were told that it was poison ivy and came out in a rash as a result. But the thing is, their arms were actually rubbed with a maple leaf. The belief itself was enough to stimulate a histamine reaction. Another group of volunteers was told that their arms were being rubbed with a maple leaf, but it really *was* poison ivy this time. But they didn't come out in a rash at all, even though they were all allergic to poison ivy. Their belief had overpowered their normal allergic reaction. Of course, I'm not saying that poison ivy doesn't cause an allergic reaction – we know that it does. What I *am* suggesting is that the mind is able to overrule it.

The mind has far more ability to overpower the body's programming than most people think. I have heard many people say that the reason they are easily stressed is genetic – their mother or father was highly strung so they can't help it. It may be that they have inherited a genetic or epigenetic tendency to get stressed easily, but this doesn't mean that they are destined to be stressed for life. A regular practice of yoga or meditation is usually enough to calm them down, even under exactly the same conditions in which they were stressed before. Harvard University research on meditation demonstrated that it impacted 1,561 genes in people who had never meditated before, activating 874 genes and deactivating 687.[13] That's some effect!

So, there are genetic currents of destiny – some that are inherited as normal from our parents, and others that are a consequence of their experiences in life. But our choices in life can overrule many of these effects. Yes, the river has a current, but our boat doesn't always need to flow with it.

******

So far in the book we've looked at some of the forces that influence us. We've seen how cycles of the Earth, sun, and moon can set us on a current of destiny, and even how our ancestors' experiences can have an effect on us. We've also learned how we can make choices to overrule them.

In the next chapter, we change focus altogether. Rather than looking at the past and present, we will consider how the body seems to be able to sense future events before they occur. Does this mean the future is set in stone?

KEY POINTS

- We inherit the effects of our parents' and our grandparents' life experiences.

- Their experiences leave an epigenetic mark, like an emblem, on their genes.

- Our life experiences can overrule or reprogram the epigenome.

- The mind is a powerful tool in changing our life.

LIFE EXPERIMENTS

- What healthy changes can you make in your life right now?

- Commit to making one or two of these changes in the next three days.

CHAPTER 4

SENSING THE FUTURE

'I feel there are two people inside me – me and my intuition. If I go against her, she'll screw me every time, and if I follow her, we get along quite nicely.'

KIM BASINGER

A few years ago Elizabeth's mother, Elma, seemingly randomly spoke about an old friend she hadn't seen, or even thought about, in around 20 years. The very next day, the friend arrived at her door, right out of the blue. She was in the area and just thought she'd pop in and say hello.

Have you ever just thought of someone and then they appeared, or just known something was going to happen and then it did?

There are many terms for this kind of thing, from 'intuition' and 'ESP,' to 'psi,' and 'being psychic,' but regardless of the words we use, the phenomenon hints at a reality somewhat different from what we currently understand in science. I have personally found that scientific friends are more accepting of it when it is called 'intuition.' But whatever the language we use, we do seem to be able to sense things ahead of time.

THE THREE PATHS OF INTUITION

I'll use the term 'intuition' here. The word was first used in the fifteenth century and referred to 'mentally looking at' something. But in the seventeenth century its meaning evolved to refer broadly to a 'sixth sense,' 'spiritual perception,' or 'hunch.' The modern use of the word encapsulates this meaning, but also includes the ability to get a sense of something in other ways. I'd like to use it, therefore, because I think there are multiple ways that we can get a hunch about something.

It seems there are different types of intuition, or at least three different paths regarding how it works. Here they are:

1. Spotting Visual and Auditory Cues

On a really obvious level, most people would agree that we tend to be more intuitive when we are in a good mood. Psychology professor Barbara Fredrickson's 'Broaden and Build' theory tells us that positive emotion increases creativity and also makes us more alert to opportunities.[1]

In this creative, alert state it's as if we have expanded awareness so that we pick up more of the visual cues around us. If we have a goal, we are more likely to spot signs and pick up snippets of conversations that can help us in the pursuit of it.

Regardless of how it comes about, we are able to use our senses to get to where we want to go.

2. Mirror Neurons

The second route of intuition is present when we are in someone's company. The human brain is highly adept at reading emotions. It is also highly adept at telling when someone isn't being truthful. This is facilitated by an interconnected network of cells in the brain known as the mirror neuron system (MNS).

When a person shows emotion it is written all over their face, as they say. Smiling and frowning move particular muscles. Happiness flexes the *zygomaticus major* muscle (it pulls the lips into a smile) and the *orbicularis oculi* muscle (at the sides of the eyes), while anger flexes the *corrugator supercilli* (between the eyebrows). This is where mirror neurons come in: our mirror neuron system mirrors the muscle movements we see in others.[2] So, being with a happy person is a sure-fire way to get stimulation of our happy muscles.

How does this relate to intuition? Well, if a person is pretending they are happy but actually they're sad inside, our mirror neuron system will mirror not only their (pretend) smiles but also the subtle facial muscle movements that reflect how they really feel.

When a person tells a lie, flashes of emotion appear on their face. These might only last for a few milliseconds – too fast for the human eye to detect, but not too fast for the MNS! It mirrors the expression and feeds back into the emotional circuits in the brain, causing us to gain a subtle (intuitive) feeling of how the other person is feeling. So, when we sense someone is sad, even though they are acting happy, we might be getting an accurate picture of how they really feel.

Some people are very sensitive in this way and others are less so, which isn't surprising as we all have innate differences in skills. The differences seem to be genetic.

Lie-detector tests work on the same premise. When a person tells a lie, their nervous system shows subtle levels of stress. This can be detected using devices that measure skin conductance, which changes with micro-amounts of sweating.

Through mirror neurons it is possible to get a broad sense of what's going to happen, especially when we sense emotion building up in a person.

3. Entangled Minds

The third route of intuition is the one that might invite a little skepticism, but I'd suggest that it is a very real mechanism, perhaps predominantly masked by the other two.

A body of scientific evidence suggests that we are connected through some levels of our mind. One of my favorite studies indicating this was where researchers at Bastyr University in Seattle, Washington, USA, worked with 'emotionally bonded couples' – couples who shared a strong emotional bond.[3] One half of the couple was placed inside an MRI scanner while the other sat in a separate room. When the one in the room was startled with a visual stimulus (like a flashing light), the MRI picked up a 'flash' in the visual cortex of their partner in the scanner.

Similar experiments with an EEG have suggested that the 'interconnectedness' is strongest between people who share an emotional bond, which correlates with a lot of people's personal experience. Many people feel connected to loved ones no matter how far apart they are, and would agree that they get a sense when something is wrong with them.

This kind of thing is even apparent with some animals. In his compelling book *Dogs That Know When Their Owners Are Coming Home*, Rupert Sheldrake describes experiments where he sent a text to a dog owner and asked them to make the decision to leave the office and head home. At the instant they made their decision, a video camera set up in their home showed their dog becoming excited and moving to the window.[4]

This kind of evidence suggests that there is some form of communication that takes place from mind to mind. As well as emotional bonds being a factor, it's likely that the effect is more pronounced under some conditions than others, and also that some people are naturally more 'in tune,' so to speak, than others.

******

Regardless of what path it takes, intuition is likely to be innate. It would undoubtedly have been an evolutionary advantage to our ancestors to have a hunch that danger was near. Acting on that hunch would save their lives and thus increase the likelihood that they would pass their genes on to the next generation. In this way, nature would 'select' genes that were linked with intuition.

Maybe the lesson in this is that it is a good idea to trust our hunches – but maybe only if we're in a good mood. And of course, we also need to be a little discerning. I guess it's all about balance.

Whereas the forms of intuition above deal mostly with intuition concerning things happening now, and, with the third path, at a distance from us, let's extend this idea to intuition in time. Einstein told us that space and time were just two sides of the same coin anyway.

PRESENTIMENT

An intuitive sense of the future has been described as evidence of 'presentiment,' that is, having a sentiment – a feeling, hunch, instinct – of the future, a sort of *pre*-feeling.

Most people I've spoken to about this in conversation have said they have experienced it. It's a very common thing, and I'd say a very normal thing, even though it hasn't had much column space in the mainstream of science. But a number of intelligent scientific studies have now probed our ability to sense accurate information about the future, and the results back up the experiences of many people.

Rather than asking people about their hunches, which can be quite subjective, the researchers used the human nervous system instead. If the nervous system 'twitches,' so to speak, before a future event, it can be suggestive of a real future sense, or presentiment.

In a typical double-blind study, a person sits in front of a computer screen that randomly selects images from a database. Each image has a positive or negative emotional tone to it – like a landscape, cheerful people, a mutilated body, a violent image, or even something erotic. Devices measure the person's emotional response to the images through the activity of their autonomic nervous system (ANS). In some experiments they measure skin conductance, and in others, pupil movements, heart rate, or blood volume.[5]

In these studies, the same result repeats itself time and time again: the person's ANS reacts to the emotional tone of the image *before* the computer even selects the image to be shown to them – usually around two to five seconds before.

OK, they might be merely anticipating the next image. Their nervous system might twitch if they were to anticipate that the next image might be, say, erotic. But if that were the case then the hit rate would be no better than chance. Half the time they'd anticipate correctly and the other half they wouldn't. But in the studies the hit rate is much better than chance.

Let's take a specific example – a 1997 presentiment study at the Consciousness Research Laboratory of the University of Las Vegas, Nevada.[6] It was led by Dean Radin and involved 31 people who were shown 1,060 photos. In a published paper titled 'Unconscious Perception of Future Emotions: An experiment in presentiment,' there was a clear indication of a 'pre-sponse' to the images, as Radin called it.

The statistical gold standard of whether a result is true or not is a 'p' value of 0.05 or less. It is a measure of the likelihood of the result being chance. The 'p' value in this experiment was 0.008 – much lower – indicating it was most definitely a true result. The nervous system really does sense the future. The emotional tone of an image provoked an ANS reaction before the computer even *decided* the tone of the image.

You'd be forgiven for wondering how on Earth that could happen. Is the mind somehow bending the rules of space and time? I will come to that later, but for now I'd like to share some more evidence to whet your appetite a little more.

Radin repeated the study in 2004.[7] Now at the Institute of Noetic Sciences in Petaluma, California, he replicated it three times. In total, the replications involved 109 people and 3,709 separate trials. Again the results clearly demonstrated presentiment. The odds of it being chance – where the nervous system just anticipated the photos – were 10,000 to one.

Interestingly, the ANS response was higher before emotional photos than before calm ones, which isn't really surprising in that we tend to react more to emotional images than to neutral ones. In purely classical terms (not looking at presentiment), it is known, for instance, that a person's emotional response is typically higher if they are presented with an image of violence than an image of, say, a nice landscape. So why would it be different with presentiment?

The Institute of HeartMath, in Boulder Creek, Colorado, echoed the results of Radin's experiments.[8] Following a similar protocol, they used the human heart as their detector rather than the skin or the pupils of the eye. In their study, 30 calm and 15 emotionally arousing pictures were shown to 26 volunteers and the heart rate of the volunteers changed more prior to future emotional images than calm ones.

The HeartMath researchers also discovered that the effect was stronger in women than in men, which might correlate with many people's experiences that women tend to be more intuitive than men.

Indeed, if empathy is a reflection of intuition (empathy has been defined as 'I feel *with* you'), then women are around 7 percent more empathetic than men.[9] This is a generalization, of course, because many men are highly empathetic and many women not so.

As you might expect, though, it's not just emotive images that can be used to measure a presentiment effect. In 2003, two physicists from the Laboratories for Fundamental Research in Palo Alto, California, exposed people to random noise, which they called 'audio startle stimuli.'[10]

In their experiment, rather than calm or violent images, there was a 50 percent chance that there would either be an audio startle or a period of silence.

The scientists measured clear ANS reactions, which were not due to anticipation of a sound, around three seconds before a random generator randomly chose an audio startle or a control period of silence. The results were highly statistically significant, with a 'p' value of 0.00054.

The results of some of the presentiment experiments seemed to show higher responses for negative or emotive content. This ability would also have been advantageous to our ancient ancestors as they set the tone of human evolution. Sensing danger, even when there were no visual signs or other people around with fear written on their faces, would have been to their advantage. Individuals particularly adept at this would have been more likely to survive and therefore pass their genes on to the next generation. Thus nature would have 'selected' genes that correlated with the ability to sense the future, especially for negative or emotive events. Maybe this is why there are far more premonitions of disaster in the world than there are premonitions of Scotland winning the soccer World Cup.

Of course, the rational mind will always seek to explain phenomena like this purely in terms of visual cues. And, of course, visual and auditory cues do play a role in many of our personal experiences of presentiment. The brain will easily be able to predict what's most likely to occur in the next few seconds by calculating the trajectory of events. That's just common sense.

But, as we can see from the scientific studies, presentiment can happen when there is no possibility of any visual cues: the experimental set-up eliminated them.

Presentiment is suggestive of the third path of intuition – and it extends to time as well as space. Our everyday experience usually involves the first and second paths, and this is why we tend to assume that they can explain every example of intuition and presentiment. The third pathway probably only rears its head from time to time, possibly when we get our mind out of the way, or when there's an emotional occurrence in the life of someone to whom we're strongly emotionally bonded.

My friend Tyson recently told me that, when he was in New York, his watch stopped. He said he felt 'strange' and immediately thought of his grandmother, who was back in the UK. The next day he learned that she had died, at approximately the time his watch had stopped.

In a variation of the above experiments, Holger Klintman, at Lund University in Sweden, used the well-known Stroop test, where a person is presented with a word which is the name of a color but is also in color and often not the color of the word.[11] So the word 'yellow' might be colored red, for instance. The test is that the person has to say the actual color, not the name of the color.

I first met this test in a 'Brain Training' program for the Nintendo DS. My first attempt suggested that my brain age was 80, although with a little practice I got it down to 79. I do recommend it; I use my brain trainer a lot. I especially like the section where you have to do 20 short calculations as fast as you can. I'm down to 12 seconds, which is really just how fast I can write on the screen.

In Klintman's study, volunteers would see a color patch and then the word of a color a few seconds later. Then they were timed to see how long it took them to say the color of the patch and then the word. Sometimes the word that followed matched the patch, and sometimes it didn't.

Interestingly, if the following word matched the color of the patch (it was *congruent*) it turned out that the volunteers could easily say the name of the patch when it was first shown to them. But here's the thing: if the following word *didn't* match the color of the patch (it was *incongruent*), the volunteers were much slower at saying the color of the patch in the first place. Their ability seemed to depend on which word would be presented a few seconds later, even though the word chosen was random and hadn't been selected at the time they were shown the patch.

Klintman called the effect 'time reversed interference' because it seemed to show that some foreknowledge of the word in the future affected the volunteers' ability to verbalize the color in the present. It was as if information was moving backward through time and interfering with their mental ability in the present.

In reference to a piece of presentiment research performed by psychologist Dick Bierman, a UK *Daily Mail* article in 2007 quoted Brian Josephson, a winner of the 1973 Nobel Prize for physics, as saying:

> *So far, the evidence seems compelling. What seems to be happening is that information is coming from the future. In fact, it's not clear in physics why you can't see the future. In physics, you certainly cannot completely rule out this effect...*
>
> *I believe that we can sense the future. We just haven't yet established the mechanism allowing it to happen. People have so-called "paranormal" or "transcendental" experiences along these lines. Bierman's work is another piece of the jigsaw. The fact that we don't understand something doesn't mean that it doesn't happen.*[12]

I found the last line particularly interesting: 'The fact that we don't understand something doesn't mean that it doesn't happen.' It is too easy to dismiss things that don't seem possible on first hearing of them – like my scientist colleague who pointed out that chronobiology 'reeked of astrology' – so perhaps we would do well to be open-minded in life. Of course, this doesn't mean believing everything we hear, but simply listening first and then checking out the evidence ourselves.

ANIMAL PRESENTIMENT

Presentiment even occurs in animals. For example, many of us are familiar with reports that animals seem to anticipate natural disasters.

In fact, prior to the Asian tsunami on December 26, 2004, there were widespread reports of animals – dogs, monkeys, elephants – running for high ground hours before the tsunami struck.

I was presenting research of this kind at a seminar recently, and a woman asked if she could share something with the audience. It transpired that her friend had been on an elephant ride in Thailand on that day in 2004, and the elephant had suddenly become agitated and run for the hills. The woman couldn't get off because she was high up and the elephant was moving really fast so, terrified, she just clung on. Once the elephant reached high ground it slowed down and stopped and she was able to get off. But she had an odd sense of danger and didn't go back down. The tsunami struck a few hours later, wiping out the entire area where she had been staying. Being on the elephant had saved her life.

Animals undoubtedly have an innate awareness of visual cues that is much more honed than ours is, given that they are much closer to nature than we are, but we can't rule out presentiment as well, especially if we consider the following experiment.

Chester Wildey, an electrical engineering student at the University of Texas at Arlington who was working on his Master's thesis in 2001, figured that if presentiment was an innate ability in all animals, including humans, he should be able to find it even in simple life forms. So he did a study over 231 trials with earthworms.[13] And, just as in the human presentiment experiments, he discovered that earthworms reacted ahead of time. Rather than showing them images, which I'm not sure would mean that much to earthworms, he used different types of vibration, since earthworms can navigate by feeling vibrations.

He found that earthworms have a 'presentiment window' – the period of time that the nervous system senses an event before it occurs – of about one second. You'll remember that it was around two to five seconds in humans. This doesn't mean that we only sense information two to five seconds ahead of time; it only means that it was two to five seconds under those particular experimental conditions.

REMOTE VIEWING INTO THE FUTURE

We have much longer presentiment windows with remote viewing, which is where a person tries to see what is happening in a different location. In a typical remote-viewing experiment, a person goes to a location that is randomly selected from a database and a remote viewer (the receiver) has to sense where they are.

Formal research into remote viewing began in California at the Stanford Research Institute (SRI), an institute founded in 1946 by Stanford University and a group of west coast industrialists as part of client-sponsored research and development for government, private, and nonprofit institutions. The remote viewing was part of a CIA-funded program that started in the early 1970s.[14]

In his 1996 memoir of remote-viewing research at the SRI, Russell Targ wrote the following:

> In 1974 Hal Puthoff and I had set aside our careers as laser physicists and were conducting viewing experiments at SRI, supported largely by the CIA. One of the many assignments we received was to describe a Soviet research and development laboratory at a particular latitude and longitude in the USSR. The psychic description that we and our viewer provided to our sponsor was so outstanding that it alone assured our funding for the next several years. The results were, of course, classified at a very high level because our drawings and descriptions were verified by satellite photography.[15]

Much of Puthoff and Targ's work involved a remote viewer named Ingo Swann, who was found to be particularly adept at it. In one paper, Puthoff wrote:

To determine whether it was necessary to have a 'beacon' individual at the target site, Swann suggested carrying out an experiment to remote view the planet Jupiter before the upcoming NASA Pioneer 10 flyby. In that case, much to his chagrin (and ours), he found a ring around Jupiter, and wondered if he had perhaps remote viewed Saturn by mistake. Our colleagues in astronomy were quite unimpressed as well, until the flyby revealed that an unanticipated ring did in fact exist.[16]

When their entire pool of remote-viewing research was combined, the statistics were highly impressive. The odds against their hits being chance were found to be 1 billion billion (10^{18}) to one. Also, after several years of their own remote-viewing research, Princeton University, New Jersey, scientists reported odds against chance of 1 billion to one.

What most people familiar with the research aren't aware of is that remote viewers regularly identify where the target is located several hours or even days before the location is selected, sometimes just as a feeling or even in a dream.

So it would seem quite clear that we have the ability to sense the future. Exactly how that occurs isn't apparent, although that isn't going to deter me from attempting an explanation later on. And, although I've referred to it as an ability, I don't think that's the right term – it's just something that we do, in the same way that we don't call breathing an ability.

I think many of us have had instances of this in our personal lives, and I would say that we shouldn't be quick to dismiss these as chance, luck, or coincidence. Maybe we should start to accept that we are all psychic (or highly intuitive; you can choose your preferred word) in this sense, and that we can and do sense the future.

So the obvious question I sense arising in your mind is: if we can sense the future, does that mean it is predestined?

IS THE FUTURE WRITTEN IN STONE?

The answer, as far as I understand it, is 'no.' It's kind of 'yes' too, in a weird sort of way, but I'll deal with the 'no' part now and return to the 'yes' part later on.

The point is, if we can sense the future, can we change it? What if we sense something we don't like? You might have spotted an answer to that question already when I described how we might have evolved the capacity for presentiment. If an ancient ancestor sensed potential danger and therefore turned and ran away (possibly where I inherited my ability to run fast from), he was, in effect, changing the future that he sensed. He might have sensed being eaten by a large animal with big teeth, but because he ran away, he never saw it. In this way, according to evolution by natural selection, nature would have selected the genes for sensing the future (as well as those for running fast).

If we didn't have the ability to change the 'future' (I put this in inverted commas because I believe there is more than one possible future), presentiment wouldn't have any genetic correlation at all, and therefore we wouldn't have it today. As the stats show we do have it, we must have evolved it, and therefore we can change the future. Well, that's a relief!

Following a couple of interpretations of quantum physics – the Copenhagen interpretation,[17] which says that our choices eliminate other options, and the many worlds interpretation,[18] which postulates that there are parallel worlds (or universes) and each choice we make selects one of them – we can think of the future as 'probabilistic.' This means that the future we experience is only one of several probabilities (or possibilities, if you prefer) that have some likelihood of occurring.

Following this line of reasoning, we could then say that we (and animals) don't sense *the* future, but that we sense the *most likely* future. But what does that actually mean?

Imagine you are at a fork in the road and, rather than there just being two paths ahead of you, there are several. Due to your momentum, as well as the forces of destiny discussed earlier, and also taking into account your current state of mind, you can dismiss most of the paths. They are improbable. There are only really a couple of paths that have any real likelihood of you choosing them. And there will probably be one that is most likely of all.

To get the time-reversed influence that I described earlier, where information is moving backward through time, all of the paths must actually exist somewhere or 'somewhen.' This suggests to me that the many worlds interpretation might be pointing us in the right direction in terms of understanding the nature of reality. We experience presentiment of the path we are on – the most probable one – until we make a different choice; then we experience presentiment of the new path, as it becomes the most probable one. Could there be parallel realities? I'll come to that later, unless you're already inhabiting that parallel reality and are reading my future words now. I hope you enjoyed the book!

In a presentiment experiment, the future must already exist for it to communicate with the present, otherwise we'd just be anticipating it, which we already know is not the case. I would actually go as far as to say that this kind of thing is happening all the time. We're always receiving information from the future. You're doing it right now in fact!

What you're actually doing is selecting from probable futures according to how you're feeling right now. You will tend to take the most probable path. Chances are that path will be brighter than the others most of the time and make the others seem pale by comparison, like a weaker wash of a watercolor on a canvas. But the fact that the fork in the road exists means that there is always an element of choice. We just don't always notice that we can choose, or that we are always choosing for that matter.

Most people, most of the time, are actually selecting their future path based upon their interpretation of their past. It's been said that we think roughly 100,000 thoughts a day but 90,000 of them are the same ones we thought yesterday.[19] If our thinking governs our actions then it's no surprise that momentum carries us more or less along the same path we have been on in the past, at least until something different happens in our life or we actually *do* make a different choice. I like the term 'deep change or slow death,' coined by Robert E. Quinn, a professor of business administration at Michigan State University.[20] Unless we make deep changes, we tend to walk the same road in life, which for many of us isn't so great. We need to make deep changes to break momentum. And that applies to the world as well as to our personal life.

I have thought about this from a health perspective. Someone with a poor diet who doesn't take any exercise is at higher risk of cardiovascular disease than average, yet they continue to make the same (poor) dietary and lifestyle choices every day. Once they develop cardiovascular disease, it forces them into a different way of thinking so that their life then unfolds along a different path.

I once met a man who had a sense that he had some form of cardiovascular problem. He would often get an image in his mind which could relate to a cardiovascular problem. So he made some deep changes in his life, improving his diet and taking much more exercise. He never did develop the disease. That was several years ago. He changed his apparent destiny, the path he was on at the time.

In the thoroughly informative book *The Power of Premonitions*, Larry Dossey, MD, shares a story from one of his patients who dreamed that a chandelier fell on top of her baby's crib in the next room. She was startled awake and shared the dream with her husband, who assured her it was only a dream and that she should go back to sleep. In the dream it was 4:35 a.m. and the weather was stormy. The husband pointed out that the weather was calm. But the woman was still unsettled and, once her husband had gone back to sleep, she got up, took the baby from the crib and brought it into bed with her.

She was later startled awake again, this time by the actual crashing of the chandelier on top of the cot. It was 4:35 a.m. and the weather was stormy.

Did she sense the most probable future but make a different choice? I believe that she did. Both probable futures always existed. She just chose one over the other.

It's easy to dismiss this kind of thing as anecdotal, but anecdotal evidence often forms the basis of serious research. As Larry Dossey pointed out, 'An old saying in medicine makes the point: "If you don't like a patient's story you call it an anecdote. If you like it you call it a case history."'

******

In a real way, as we change our minds we change the future – or select a different future – only we don't notice, because how would we know? But it still begs the question: was I meant to make that change?

This is a question that has been asked for millennia, and I suspect we will still be debating it 1,000 years from now. We might never know the answer for sure. But as long as we feel that our choices do shape our future, does it really matter? Isn't it just a philosophical argument that has no actual bearing on life?

My answer has always been that, whatever we do, we should just do it with kindness. I like Albert Schweitzer's take on this. He wrote, 'I don't know what your destiny will be, but one thing I know: the only ones among you who will be happy are those who have sought and found how to serve.'

63

But for now, to continue with our exploration of whether life is mapped out or not, we need also to explore how our thinking influences our experiences in life, and also how it is possible that we can sense future events before they occur.

KEY POINTS

- There are three different pathways through which intuition works: i) spotting visual and auditory cues; ii) mirror neurons, and iii) entangled minds.

- Lots of research shows that we have the ability to sense the future. It is known as *presentiment*.

- Presentiment is a natural ability that has evolved by natural selection.

- Animals have presentiment too.

- The future isn't written in stone but is based on probabilities. We can change the future.

LIFE EXPERIMENTS

- Pay attention to your intuition and notice when you are correct. This in turn will heighten your intuition because you'll stop doubting yourself.

- Try to sense who is calling you when your phone rings (before you look at the screen). See how often you are correct.

- Can you think of a time in your life when you had an instinct about something and it was right? Can you think of a time when an instinct forced you to make a change?

- Reflect on the thought that there are multiple paths ahead of you, and that you can change the future. Do you sense anything ahead of you that you'd like to change?

CHAPTER 5

THE THREE LEVELS OF CREATION

'Nothing can prevent your picture from coming into concrete form except the same power which gave it birth – yourself.'

GENEVIEVE BEHREND

As I mentioned earlier, there is no question that we can shape our lives by our intentions and actions. I can choose to have some toast by walking into the kitchen, putting bread in the toaster and then buttering the toasted bread. *Voilá*! I have created toast.

After my PhD, I worked in the pharmaceutical industry between 1995 and 1999, developing drugs for cardiovascular disease and cancer. During this time, as my understanding of the impact of the mind upon the body expanded (partly gained through a growing awareness of the placebo effect in drug trials), and my observation grew that my mind and actions shaped many of the circumstances of my life, I concluded that, even though I was a trained chemist (I trained in building molecules), we are, in fact, all chemists.

As we change our mind, so we change the chemistry of our brain and body. If we were to think of someone with whom we have had issues or challenges, and were to reflect on some of the reasons for this, we would alter our brain chemistry. As well as changing neurotransmitter concentrations in multiple brain regions, we would produce stress chemicals in the hypothalamus, which would be modified in the pituitary before being released into the bloodstream. When these chemicals reached our adrenal glands, this would lead to the production of adrenaline. We would also have elevated levels of cortisol.

If we kept thinking like this on a regular basis, we would also be likely to increase free radical levels in our bloodstream, as well as produce chemicals known as pro-inflammatory cytokines like interleukin-6 and tumor necrosis factor.

All this would only be a fraction of what would be going on. At the genetic level we would be activating and deactivating hundreds of genes.

But let's say we thought about someone we loved and felt feelings of love or compassion for them. Now we would also be modifying neurotransmitter levels in multiple brain regions, but in a different pattern. We would be producing the bonding hormone, oxytocin, too, which would actually turn down activity in the fear and anxiety part of the brain known as the amygdala. Oxytocin would be released into the bloodstream, as well as being simultaneously produced throughout the body. It would cause widening of our arteries by facilitating production of nitric oxide and a protein called atrial natriuretic peptide (ANP). At the same time, our vagus nerve would be stimulated, which would turn down genes that produced pro-inflammatory cytokines in what is known as the 'inflammatory reflex.'

We're quite the chemists! In a real way, as incredible as it might sound to some, making a conscious decision about what to focus on can have considerable effects on the chemistry, and therefore the health, of the body.

What is equally fascinating to me is that we also shape the chemistry of our life, as if the world around us is in some way an extension of our body. This is most obvious in our relationships. A person with an angry mind will somehow get themselves into more conflict situations than most people, be they in the household, in social situations, or at work, and this will interfere with the pursuit of their goals in life. A person with their mind focused on love will be likely to have more intimate relationships and better-quality friendships. They will be helped out by others, because people tend to like those who are kind. This in turn will contribute to their success as they pursue their goals.

With these types of thoughts occupying my mind during my time in the pharmaceutical industry, I daydreamed a lot about a new life writing books and giving talks. I imagined myself inspiring people, helping them to improve their lives. I also saw myself signing books and speaking at events alongside some of the people whose books I had read and been inspired by: Louise Hay, Wayne Dyer, Deepak Chopra, Tony Robbins, and others. I did this a lot because the idea so inspired me. To be honest, it was a longing. I felt more real and alive when I was dreaming about doing this than when I was doing anything in my real life.

Eventually, while I was attending a four-day 'Unleash the Power Within' seminar run by Tony Robbins in July 1999, I made the decision to resign from my job. I handed my notice in the next day, much to the shock of my boss at the time.

Now, as I fondly reflect upon this time in my life, I can see that I am living that dream. I am the author of several books and I do speak at events alongside those other authors (at least some of them).

How did it come about? How do we create, manifest, shape, or attract things in our lives? After much personal study in the field and gaining a broad awareness of some fields of science, I have concluded that there are three ways. I call these the 'three levels of creation.'

LEVEL 1: ACTION

OK, so I had to physically resign from my job. I didn't visualize my dream and then wake up the next day with a bound copy of my first book in one hand and a list of forthcoming speaking events in the other. I had to act.

Everyone has this experience. We all know that there are things that we need to do physically to shape our lives, but often, when reading up about the 'law of attraction' – the observation that we attract whatever we give most of our attention to – and similar ideas, we forget that we still have work to do. Some of us hold on to the idea that a single thought is all it takes. Sometimes that *is* the case, but most of the time we have to take some action along the way. So, to become the author I'd imagined myself to be, once I'd resigned from my job I had to physically write a book.

Depending on the goal, I'd say that action usually requires serious commitment to a direction or purpose, otherwise we lose motivation when things get tough, or we just run round in circles. A demonstration of commitment can be a powerful thing, because it helps us to get really clear in our own mind exactly what it is we are trying to achieve. The clearer the focus, the better the chance of achieving the goal.

Psychologist and bestselling author Robert Holden shared an analogy in his book *Success Intelligence.*[1] He described a scene from the British comedy series *Monty Python's Flying Circus* of the '100 meter dash for people with no sense of direction.' When the gun goes off, the athletes all run in random directions with no one actually heading toward the finish line.

I was absolutely committed to writing my first book. I had a crystal-clear sense of purpose, so I had to make the time to write, regardless of everything else that was going on in my life at the time. In the end, I wrote the bulk of the book in the middle of the night, because it was the only time I could actually find.

I didn't begin writing it until a few years after I had left the pharmaceutical industry in the end, because I side-stepped toward another goal, which was to set up and run a charity. A few friends and I cofounded Spirit Aid Foundation, a charity whose mission was to help children around the world who had been affected by war and poverty. I left the charity a little over two years later and then started writing.

To earn a living in the meantime, I took two teaching jobs; teaching mostly chemistry, but also classes in ecology and mathematics. My teaching schedule meant that there were some days when I didn't have a class until the afternoon, so I'd switch on my laptop at about 11 p.m. the night before and write until around 3:30 a.m. I did that for several months. It wasn't easy, although I did really enjoy the experience and have fond memories of it when I think back. There was something ceremonial, almost magical, about making a pot of coffee, lighting some candles and playing some inspiring music as I wrote in the stillness of the night. So, despite the late hours and the teaching job, my commitment meant that the book got written.

Action is crucial for the crystallization of most of our goals, and it usually takes commitment.

I have had to take many more actions since then. Getting published wasn't exactly a cakewalk. The ten UK publishers I sent my manuscript to all rejected it. I was feeling dejected after that and thought my dream had died, but my partner Elizabeth convinced me that I should self-publish. I remember her saying, in her typically fiery, spirited manner, 'What do they know anyway? How many great books were turned down by loads of publishers? It's all just opinion.' She was absolutely right! That thought gave me a renewed sense of purpose, so I self-published. Another action!

About six months after I self-published, the book was accepted by Hay House UK, but even that required action in that I had to physically contact them.

As a public speaker, I've also had to take action: I've had to get out and actually *do* talks! Between 2008 and 2011, I averaged 120–150 speaking events a year as I learned my craft, so to speak.

I could write a whole book about the number of actions I've had to take in my life, and I'm still taking now, but this isn't an autobiography (yet). I'm using personal examples because I hope you will identify with the situations I have personally been in, and I want to show that each of us has personal actions to take in the pursuit of our dreams.

If we were all told our destiny in advance, would we try as hard? I don't think so. I'm writing these words after watching Rafael Nadal become the first player to win the French Open Tennis Championship seven times. It was a tough match, as he had to overcome Novak Djokovic, world number one and holder of the other three majors leading into the French Open. If 'Rafa' had known that his destiny was to win seven titles (or more), would he have worked as hard as he did? Maybe, but I don't think he would have – and then he might not have won the match after all. So maybe it's best that we don't know our destiny. In fact, I think that destiny is often created through the hard work of mastering our craft.

Things can just happen, of course. In my own life there have been many occasions when things just seemed to happen without any work on my part. But a lot of the time, I had to act to become the person I needed to be in order to take advantage of those unexpected opportunities.

Sometimes it's all in the timing, too. I doubt I could have spoken in front of 4,000 people ten years ago with the same passion, humor, and confidence as I do now. I have grown into that person, and I'm still growing. It has been a journey filled with action!

LEVEL 2: THE PRINCIPLE OF INTERCONNECTEDNESS

I call the second level of creation the 'principle of interconnectedness.' It is through this principle that many opportunities present themselves to us.

We're interconnected in two main ways that are relevant to shaping our lives. The first is through our social networks.

Interconnectedness through Social Networks

We are all embedded in social networks. We have friends, family members, colleagues, and contacts who all have other friends, family members, colleagues, and contacts. Together, we form an intricate web, and one, crucially, through which information flows just as electricity flows through a copper wire.

Through this web we share knowledge, information, contacts, inspiration, humor, and know-how. All of these things occur through socially connecting with one another. If you are really honest with yourself, I'll bet that few (possibly none) of your achievements in life have come about through your efforts alone. Most will have involved at least some degree of connecting with other people, even if it was just a supportive chat.

For example, my move from self-published to publisher-published author was aided by the friend of a friend. Alisoun McKenzie and her business partner had actually invited me out to dinner to discuss corporate workshops. I don't usually make a habit of telling people my goals, especially the important ones, but during our conversation, prompted by Alisoun's openness, I felt compelled to mention that I had decided that I wanted to be published, and that I'd love it to be by Hay House. Alisoun, it turned out, had a friend who was a Hay House author and had actually helped out on their stand at a book fair. She gave me the e-mail address of the marketing director. One thing led to another, as they say, and I was signed up a few weeks later.

One thing that helped my case was listing my book sales, and the large majority had occurred at speaking events, many of which had been organized by my friend Mary McPherson – another social connection!

This isn't the only way that opportunities come to us, though. There is a much more subtle form of interconnectedness out there that's not exactly endorsed by mainstream science...

Interconnectedness as a Basic Property of Reality

If you were to peer inside the atoms that comprise your body, or anything solid for that matter, you would learn that they were mostly empty space. In fact, an atom is about 99.9999999999999 percent empty space. If one of its protons were the size of a grape, then one of its electrons would be the size of a grain of sand and be nearly 3 km (2 miles) away. And inside the protons there is even more empty space. If fact, the ratio of 'space' to 'stuff' is simply breathtaking.

An interesting property of the subatomic world is entanglement,[2] which is where subatomic particles can be connected – or entangled – at great distances, seemingly disobeying the cosmic speed limit set down by Einstein. This can occur instantly in time *and* space, in what is called a 'non-local' connection.

Most physicists and cosmologists now agree that all particles were entangled at the beginning of time, and therefore they remain entangled today. What this means is that everything in the entire universe is interconnected – including you and me, a leaf on a tree in a distant forest, a grain of dust on the surface of the moon, a rock on one of Saturn's rings, and even a grain of dust in a distant nebula over 1.6 trillion km (1 trillion miles) away. We can actually think of the whole universe as a single organism.

The interconnectedness through entanglement is where subatomic particles are 'correlated,' meaning if one becomes polarized horizontally, the other instantly takes up a vertical polarization, even if they are a trillion kilometers apart. The distance is irrelevant. The second particle just seems to 'know' the state of the other: they are correlated.

This doesn't exactly mean that information can be sent from one distant part of the universe to another like a text message, but it does mean that there are subtle connections that we're only just beginning to probe and understand.

It definitely appears that what happens to a single particle is *felt* on some level by the entire universe. That means that the universe 'knows' everything about each of us. Wow! What a concept!

This is where we need to take a side-step away from mainstream science and take a more esoteric view of interconnectedness in order to understand how information can and does transmit.

The pioneering psychologist Carl Gustav Jung discussed the idea of a collective unconscious – that at a deep level of the psyche we overlap, as it were, with one another and are thus interconnected. I like to think of it as something like the internet. We can have computers on our desks at home and at work, and they are clearly separate from each other, just as you and I are clearly separate from each other. But when they are connected to the internet, although they have physically separate parts, they are also part of an interconnected network – a collective repository of information – where information freely flows from one to another. We might think of ourselves in the same way – as clearly separate 'parts,' but sharing information on some level: the level of the collective unconscious mind, to use Jung's idea.

A nice metaphor would be a spider's web. Each of us is a node on the web, and the strands represent our interconnections. How does a spider know when a fly is trapped in its web? It feels the vibrations. So, in some way, the entire universe feels the vibrations (or waves of information) from all of our movements, thoughts, emotions, and even hopes and dreams.

I believe that meaningful information is always being sent out in this way. In other words, if you have a hope or a dream, the universe and everyone in it knows about it on some level.

You might notice the parallels between the idea of entanglement – where the universe 'feels' your movements – and the collective unconscious, or entanglement of consciousness. Interconnectedness is a fractal phenomenon in that it repeats itself at different scales. It is preserved throughout all levels of reality, from the interconnection of subatomic particles to the interplay between atoms, molecules, the human nervous system, human relationships, the planets in the solar system, and superclusters of galaxies connected through mass gravitational fields. Why, then, should there be any difference with the connection between minds?

This is an impossible idea to accept if you take the standard view in science: that consciousness is an 'epiphenomenon' in that it emerges out of the complexity and density of wiring in the brain, almost like a side effect. But there is a great deal of published research and philosophy that challenges *that* idea.

I have no doubt that our self-awareness is *correlated* with the complexity of brain wiring, but I wouldn't say that it is *caused* by it. There is actually no scientific proof that consciousness is an epiphenomenon, despite the way the idea is promoted in the mainstream. The lack of scientific understanding of what consciousness actually is, and where it comes from, is referred to in the scientific community as the 'hard' problem.

My contention is that consciousness is not confined inside the head, but is a fundamental property of reality, and it is from this position that I will be discussing many of the ideas around destiny and free will. Consciousness, according to this premise, is able to span space and also time. This therefore allows us to accept the evidence of presentiment, rather than dismiss it, which is what a belief in epiphenomenalism forces us to do (unless the mind is able to pick up backward time signals, which might be possible).

Here are a few published scientific experiments that lend support to the idea that consciousness is not confined inside the head.

In a classic experiment, a person attempts to send thoughts (usually pictures) to a person who is asleep. The theory is that the sleeping person will pick the thoughts and pictures up in their dreams. In 2003, after analyzing 47 separate dream experiments that involved 1,270 individual trials, British psychologists Simon Sherwood and Chris Roe of University College Northampton found that the overall accuracy in receiving a picture was 59.1 percent.[3] According to chance, it should have been 50 percent. The odds of the results of the experiment being chance were calculated at an astronomical 22 billion to one.

In a different experiment, conducted at Scotland's Edinburgh University in 2004 with 26 couples, ten randomly paired strangers and five people who weren't paired with anyone but thought they were (therefore unknowingly doing the experiment alone, to serve as a control), a correlation was found in the EEG rhythms between pairings. When one person was startled, the brain of their partner was affected too, even though they were either in different rooms or, if in the same room, shielded from each other. The researchers found a match between the couples, as you might expect because of their emotional connection, but they also found a connection between the non-related people, although it was weaker. There was no change in the electrical activity of the brain with the unmatched people.

Similarly, in 2004 at the Institute of Noetic Sciences, senior scientist Dean Radin and some of his colleagues tested 13 sets of friends who were not emotionally bonded as couples, but shared an interest in the study. One person in each pair (the receiver) was connected to an EEG machine, and a closed-circuit TV camera was pointed at them. The other (the sender) sat in front of a TV screen in another room and was also connected to an EEG machine. At randomly timed intervals the sender's TV screen flashed up a live image of the receiver's face. The EEG machine connected to the sender showed a peak, as you might expect with the sudden appearance of their friend's face on the screen, but the receiver's EEG also showed a peak, demonstrating a connection between them. It was almost as though the receiver sensed that someone was looking at them.

Dean Radin reported the above studies in his informative and provocative book *Entangled Minds*.[4] I would recommend it to anyone seeking scientific evidence of our interconnectedness.

If we accept this evidence, it means that, even though we appear to be physically separate from one another, our thoughts, emotions, hopes, dreams, and intentions might travel between us just as information flows between us in social networks. Could this help us to achieve what we want? I would say that it does.

How I think a lot of life actually works is that our hopes and dreams are sent out like requests for help. It's as if we're broadcasting signals. People pick up these signals and make unconscious choices that cause them to meet us at just the right time to help us or, if they are people we already know, they are perhaps moved to say something or do something at a particular moment.

Some people might say that these occurrences are just random, and that of course we will get meaningful information some of the time from those around us. That is absolutely true, but it doesn't rule out attracting people in this way.

Grateful to a Jumbo

I'd like to share a little experience that I had that I can only explain from the viewpoint of interconnectedness.

A few years ago I was thrilled to get my first invitation to speak at one of Hay House's 'I Can Do It' conferences. It was to be held in Las Vegas, USA. But, despite my initial excitement, fears began to arise in me at the thought of flying.

Our last flight across the Atlantic had involved more turbulence than either Elizabeth or I had ever known. Despite my training, positive thinking had gone right out of the window, and I hadn't been helped by Elizabeth telling me of her vivid dream the night before of our plane crashing into the ocean.

I felt traumatized after that flight and developed a fear of flying for the next few years. Elizabeth thought it was funny that on subsequent flights my hands would go ice-cold.

Fortunately, when I got my conference invitation, I was able to comfort myself with some visualization, although not in the way you might think. I visualized myself standing beside the plane I was to fly on, with my hands on the nacelles (the area housing the engines), saying a prayer of gratitude to the plane for getting us safely to our destination. I imagined this several times.

A few months or so later, I was giving a talk at a conference in London and had the sudden urge to talk about research into interconnectedness. I even explored some of the research that I will discuss later in this book, where consciousness can seemingly interact with physical things. I explained that our car was called Charlotte, and that I often said thanks to her for getting us to our destination time and time again – and how I believed, silly as it might sound, that it helped in some way. I hadn't planned on saying these things to the rather large audience at all, but sometimes you just feel that you can talk about some deeper subjects!

After my lecture, a woman approached me and said she had loved my talk but the one thing that had most resonated with her was the idea that I said thanks to my car. She said, *'I'm an airline pilot, and before every flight I place my hands on the nacelles of the plane and say a prayer of gratitude to it for the forthcoming flight.'* She went on, *'The cabin crew think it's quite spooky that we rarely seem to get turbulence on the flights and also rarely have any angry or difficult passengers.'* That was when the hairs on the back of my neck stood up.

I didn't tell her of my visualization, but joked that I wished she was the pilot on my next flight. That's when she said, *'That would only happen if you were flying to Las Vegas!'*

It turned out that she was one of a few captains who flew the London to Las Vegas route, the exact route I was to fly on. For the next few months or so we were e-mailing each other as she was trying to find out if she would be on my flight. It turned out that she wasn't – it was another captain's 50th birthday and he was celebrating with friends and family in Las Vegas, so he piloted us that day – but that didn't make the experience any less incredible for me.

Rather than dismiss such 'coincidences' as random, what if we were to consider that life really does work in this way? This kind of thinking has led me personally to a much more meaningful way of looking at reality and the interactions between people.

LEVEL 3: EMBEDDED CONSCIOUSNESS

The third level of creation is where things take on a mystical twist.

We know that it's mostly empty space once we get to the subatomic level, but the kind of space I mentioned is relatively large in comparison to the smallest scale we're aware of. Called the 'Planck scale,' after Max Planck, one of the founders of quantum mechanics, it is the scale of 10^{-35} meters. A meter is 10^0 (i.e. 1), a centimeter is 10^{-2} (that's 0.01 meters), a millimeter is 10^{-3} (0.001 meters), and so on. A nanometer is 10^{-9} (0.000000001 meters) and an atom is approximately 10^{-10} (0.0000000001 meters), so you can begin to appreciate the tiny scale we're talking about.

The Planck scale is the basic fabric of reality, as far as we know. No one has actually observed it, because we can't probe such a small scale. The number pops out of mathematical equations that describe the physical laws.

Consciousness might be stitched into reality at the Planck scale, or even beyond if such a space exists. I believe that the idea that consciousness is a fundamental property of reality is the best way to account for the experimental evidence that I have discussed so far, and the *experiential* evidence of ordinary people. Rather than being a product of brain chemistry, consciousness is a field of energy or information that is everywhere and in everything. Of course, that is speculation.

To speculate further, what we experience as our own consciousness is consciousness that is localized (or focused) on our own body, just as a subatomic particle exists where the quantum field is said to be more intense.

Consciousness is therefore in everything around us, though clearly it's not the same kind of consciousness as we have. I wouldn't say that a wall has self-aware consciousness, but there must be consciousness there all the same. Following this idea through, even an atom has consciousness, which is the basic idea behind the philosophy of panpsychism.

I think one of the reasons why this idea might resonate with many people is because it is the basic principle taught by a number of spiritual and wisdom traditions around the world. It is also an idea central to many religions, although perhaps in some cases it has become a little lost among the moral teachings and rules for living.

There are valid scientific objections to the idea that consciousness is anything other than a product of the brain. But the assumption that it is produced by the brain should raise similar objections. For instance, a radio or TV doesn't create sound or images, it *receives* signals from outside, which it processes to give us the sound or picture. Damaging some of the wires or circuits in the radio or TV would interfere with the sound or picture, but this doesn't mean that the sound or picture is created by the radio or TV. Yet the standard wisdom cites the fact that damage to brain circuits affects consciousness as proof that the brain *produces* consciousness.

Perhaps instead we can think of the brain as a radio or TV that receives consciousness (or some form of conscious information) from outside and then processes it so that we have self-awareness and the ability to perceive the world, think, and communicate.

When there's damage to some of the brain circuits, the signal is affected, and so self-awareness and the ability to perceive, think, and communicate are hampered. The brain doesn't need to *produce* consciousness for this to happen, though – it only needs to receive it and process it.

If consciousness is part of reality then it means that we are already intimately connected with what we want – it is, in some ways, part of us. Bringing it into our lives involves attracting it to ourselves via resonating with it through our thoughts. The problem is that many of us give as much, or more, attention to what we don't want in life as to what we do want. The net effect is like being pulled two different ways and not really going anywhere. Sound familiar?

The obvious objection to this is that we are therefore to blame for everything bad that happens to us, because everything is our creation. But we already know that some of life is influenced by forces outside ourselves, and I will discuss the internal forces that can influence us later in the book. It's not all our fault.

From observations of my own life, I conclude that we move toward what we focus on. So, regardless of whether our thoughts and actions are predestined or not, we still create our personal reality.

I'd now like to delve even deeper into how we impact our own reality.

KEY POINTS

- There are three levels of creation: action, the principle of interconnectedness, and embedded consciousness.

- We need to act to move toward what we want in life.

- Information flows between us through social networks and also at a deeper level of interconnectedness.

- Consciousness is part of the fabric of reality, so we are already connected to the things we want.

- We need to give attention to what we want, not to what we don't want. We attract what we focus on.

LIFE EXPERIMENTS

- Pay attention to how you achieve your goals. Get a notebook and write down the actions you take, but also note how other people play a role. This will strengthen your understanding of how you create things in this way, and give you more faith in yourself and your abilities.

- Meditate on the idea that your mind is intimately part of the fabric of reality, and that you are connected to everything that you want and aspire to become in your life. In this meditation, focus on your hopes, dreams, and goals.

CHAPTER 6

MIND–REALITY INTERACTIONS

'I claim that human mind or human society is not divided into watertight compartments called social, political and religious. All act and react upon one another.'

GANDHI

In my opinion, the observations from experiments in presentiment and distant mind–mind interactions bring us to the profound, yet obvious in many ways, realization that our mind impacts our life far more than we think it does.

So, let's take the subject a little further and explore some other ways that our minds impact the world around us, and what that leads us to conclude about whether life is mapped out or not.

PEAR RESEARCH

The Princeton Engineering Anomalies Research (PEAR) laboratory was founded in 1979 by Robert Jahn and ran under the sponsorship of Princeton University's School of Engineering and Applied Science in New Jersey, USA, for almost three decades. The group then moved to a new home at the International Consciousness Research Laboratories (ICRL), also in Princeton, New Jersey. The PEAR lab and ICRL were both founded to explore consciousness anomalies – and, wow, were their experiments mind-blowing in their implications!

In some ways similar to the presentiment study where a person sits in front of a computer, the PEAR research was different in that, rather than sense the emotional tone of the next random image, it showed that people could actually *change* what the computer was randomly selecting. In other words, rather than sensing information coming *toward* you, the PEAR research showed that you could send information *outward* to impact the world.[1]

The PEAR lab measured the impact of a person's intention on random data, which might be binary numbers, for instance, or random sound bites, or even balls falling into holes. So a person could sit in front of a computer that was generating this random data – a random event generator (REG) – and cause it to become non-random. In other words, patterns would emerge in the numbers that could not be attributed to chance or just random clustering.

The first experiments involved a single individual who did tens of thousands of trials – and time and time again, could sway the random data. This result was then replicated thousands of times with numerous different people.

The cumulative data, now from three decades of work, is truly compelling. In fact, a meta-analysis revealed that the odds against the results being chance were in the region of 10 to the power 12 (10^{12}) to one. In summing up much of the research, the experimenters reported the following:

> In unattended calibrations, all of these sophisticated machines produced strictly random data, yet the experimental results display increases in information content that can only be attributed to the consciousness of their human operators.[2]

The experiments were done under controlled conditions involving one person and a computer or other device that generated random data. But might the effect be something that is happening in our personal lives all the time? Might we be influencing the reality around us in seemingly mystical ways? If we can influence random data produced by a machine, then we have to consider that we interact with other physical things around us too. The PEAR results hint at effects that would certainly fit the third level of creation. Going further, might it be an even larger phenomenon, where we impact world events? It's certainly something to think about.

The initial PEAR experiments mostly involved one person at a time, but the researchers have conducted experiments involving groups of people too, referring to them as 'field anomalies' and getting the best results in specific settings. They noted that:

Venues that appear to be particularly conducive to such field anomalies include small intimate groups, group rituals, sacred sites, musical and theatrical performances, and other charismatic events. In contrast, data generated during most academic conferences, business meetings, or other mundane venues showed less deviation than would be expected by chance.[3]

It seems that events that generate heightened emotion in particular produce significant results, like funeral services and even football games. Readings inside the Great Pyramid in Egypt were reportedly 'off the scale.'[4]

Scaling up even further, the researchers found effects on the REGs when millions of people were focusing on the same thing at the same time. Of course, they didn't all sit around a computer – I'm not sure there would have been enough space in a cramped lab! – these were 'unintentional' effects. They came during events that were reported on around the world – typically news items or global concerts, and even when groups coordinated mass meditations. For all of these, the REGs would show patterns above random chance. There was even a significant effect when President Obama was inaugurated, especially between 12:07 p.m. and 12:27 p.m. during his oath and speech.[5]

This research is part of the Global Consciousness Project, a PEAR spin-off that involves the collaboration of around 100 scientists and engineers from around the world. Rather than a single REG, they have REGs interfaced with computers in dozens of locations around the world. Each of them processes

200 random bits of data per second and sends all of their data to a server at Princeton University. The devices are affectionately known as 'Princeton eggs' and, as Roger Nelson, one of the principal researchers, describes it, they are 'taking the EEG of the planet.' In a 2003 interview with *The New York Times*, he said: *'Like an electroencephalogram, which measures brain activity by electrodes distributed over the surface of the head, we have sensors around the world, measuring the human population as a whole.'*[6]

In this way, the Global Consciousness Project has consistently shown that mass human consciousness impacts REG data, just as individual human consciousness impacts EEG data.

Early in the project, the researchers examined REG data at the time of the death of Princess Diana, when there was high global emotion. The resulting REG data was significant. Collectively, the odds against chance were in the region of 1 billion to one.[7]

Why should this kind of phenomenon be a surprise to us? If you think about it, the stock market is already a global indicator of mass emotion or sentiment. The PEAR research is only one step removed: it measures sentiment using random numbers rather than stock fluctuations. The difference is that with stock markets we can chart a mechanism – a series of steps – showing how global sentiment can affect stock returns. We can explain, for instance, why investors get jumpy and sell, causing stocks to fall. With the PEAR research, the mechanism hasn't quite been figured out yet.

We can actually think of stock market changes as evidence of the effect of human emotion, and therefore consciousness, but at the level of action (level 1) and social networks (level 2). PEAR research comes in at level 3.

The data strongly suggest that, both individually and *en masse*, we influence the reality around us. The results don't tell us exactly how much, just that we do. But, taken together with the three levels of creation, the research suggests that individually and collectively we are constantly creating the reality around us. There may be forces that act upon us, but we certainly shape some of what happens around us.

SENSING THE FUTURE

You might be wondering if the REG set-up could also show presentiment effects. This is where things take a turn for the even more fascinating.

ICRL researchers did indeed sometimes see REG effects *before* an event actually took place. Echoing presentiment research results, when the data for the September 11th events in New York City and the London bombings of 2005 were viewed on a graph, the REG output seemed to change a few hours before the terrorist attacks actually took place.[8] There is still some debate about whether this was a chance result or a 'real' result, but given the data already presented so far, my hunch is that it was a real phenomenon.

I have discussed this research dozens of times in public talks, and the question that most often arises in members of the audience is: could these experiments be used to forewarn governments of impending terrorist attacks? For instance, could governments cross-check REG data with secret service surveillance around the world to see if there is increased activity anywhere that might pinpoint something going on? There may well be real potential there.

Applications like this echo the book *Minority Report,* by Philip K. Dick, which was later made into a movie starring Tom Cruise. The story centers on 'pre-crime,' where three psychics sense future crime, thus enabling the law to intervene before the crime is committed and thereby prevent it.

There is a little technical challenge, though: the REG data look much the same for positive events (like mass meditations) as for terrorist attacks. The graphs just show deviations from purely random, like a mountain range rising up from flat terrain.

My contention is that the REGs pick up a 'disturbance in the field,' rather like a wave in a swimming pool. The wave would be much the same, however, whether a person made an up–down movement with their hand or a side-to-side swish. If you were standing at the other end of the pool, you would only feel a wave and wouldn't be able to discern which type of movement the person had made with their hand at the other end.

But let's not stop here – let's play with the idea a little! If we can sense the future in that consciousness can seemingly stretch forward in time and gain an impression of future events, this can also be thought of as information traveling backward from the future to the present. Therefore, we should also be able to stretch into the past, or send information into the past. Could it even be possible to flip our ideas of time on their heads? Could we actually 'remember' the future and change the past?

It sounds like a crazy idea, but presentiment research presents a case for remembering the future in that we are detecting something before it occurs, so in one sense we are remembering it because the future is happening *before* the present from our perspective. When we arrive at that future point, it is already a memory for us. I know that I'm just playing with words here, but it's to help us stretch beyond our ordinary ways of looking at things.

So, what about changing the past?

DISTANT INTENTIONALITY IN TIME RATHER THAN SPACE: CHANGING THE PAST

If I move toward a coffee cup with my hand open, do I move or does the world move toward me (assuming I'm floating at the time)? In mathematical terms it's mostly the same.

We see this type of thing in outer space. Space turns ideas of space on their heads, so to speak. An astronaut flies upward into space and reaches orbit, looking down on the Earth through a window. But, as the capsule turns round so that the window is now on the ceiling, the astronaut is now looking *up* at the world instead of down. Did he fly up into space or down?

It's the same thing – it just depends upon the perspective. If you're looking down from space at the equator and see a spaceship blast off from Antarctica, then it's clearly flying downward. But from the perspective of people standing in Antarctica, it went up all the way.

So, if the future is impacting the present through presentiment, we have to entertain the possibility that the present is impacting the past, and that the past is impacting the further past and the present – ahhhh, my head! If that is the case, we're left with an interesting paradox. Just as a person can make a choice if they receive information from the future, could a choice be made in the past if information is received from the present, even though the past has, technically, already happened?

As bizarre as it may sound, researchers have actually been studying this idea for decades. Incredibly, they have repeatedly shown that, in some ways, we seem to be writing aspects of our past from the present. It's hard to imagine this because how would we know if we were changing the past? We would always just have a memory of the past, and if the past changed, we would have a new memory.

Formal 'time-displaced' research, as it has been described, began in the early 1970s. Following research which seemed to demonstrate that we could mentally impact people and organisms at a distance in what are known as 'non-local effects,' theoretical physicist Helmut Schmidt postulated that it should also be possible to affect something that has already happened – providing that no one knew what actually *had* happened.[9]

In a typical experiment, a person would try to mentally influence random (binary) numbers to produce more ones or zeros, just as in the PEAR experiments described above. In real time, volunteers were repeatedly able to do this. Not all the time, but more times than chance would suggest – the results were statistically significant. But when Schmidt recorded the numbers a day or two earlier, and didn't tell that to the people who were trying to influence them (and he didn't know the sequence himself), they could still influence them. Incredibly, the degree of influence was about the same as it was for real-time effects, as if the numbers really were being generated at the time the volunteers attempted to influence them.

In other words, counterintuitive as it might sound, the mind is just as adept at influencing the past as it is the present. The three levels of creation must work backward in time too.

As we learned in the previous chapter, there have been hundreds of experiments where researchers have gathered evidence that it is possible for the intentions or emotions of one person to affect another person, no matter how far away they are. But as time and space are so connected, what about influencing people in the past – far away in time?

Indeed, several experiments have been done with volunteers trying to influence actual physiological readings that were recorded some time in the past. Again, the results were statistically significant – providing, again, that the volunteers didn't know the readings were prerecorded, and no one knew what the sequence was.

In 1979, for instance, Elmar Gruber, a German psychologist, used a laser known as a photobeam to record the instances of cars entering a short tunnel in Vienna during the rush hour.[10] Each car entering the tunnel would later be converted to a 'click' sound. Then, one to two months later, 'influencers' were presented with click sounds (but didn't know their source) and attempted to influence the sounds. Amazingly, they were able to influence the clicks, even though the data had been collected well over a month earlier.

In other experiments, Gruber showed 'time-displaced effects' on gerbils running on activity wheels[11], and even on people walking randomly in a dark room while listening to pink noise, which is a simulation of background noise from the environment or human biology.[12]

Not content with traffic and gerbils, Gruber also used prerecorded data of people entering a supermarket in Vienna (using a photobeam).[13] Here, too, activity was converted into click sounds, and the attempts at influencing were performed one to two months after the data were recorded. Again, there was a time-displaced effect.

What about affecting disease? Most people would immediately want to know if they could impact a disease or illness in the past. In a 1990 paper, researchers showed that a healer could slow down the spread of blood parasites in rats in the past:

Significant differences in the absolute number of infected red blood cells between experimental and control groups (both for the female and male rats) were found, possibly the result of a retroactive influence by the healer.[14]

In 1993, William Braud showed that people could retroactively affect their own ANS activity.[15] This had been recorded around half an hour earlier and was presented on a computer screen. Each influencer was invited to increase, decrease, or not influence their own electrodermal activity (EDA), the skin's ability to conduct electricity, which they thought was being produced at that moment. They succeeded.[16]

In 1997, Helmut Schmidt published research where he successfully impacted his own breathing rate in the past.[17] In the same experiment he also attempted to affect prerecorded random events. He was successful in both, but, interestingly, his scores for affecting his own biology (animate) were higher than they were for the inanimate events. It was as if he was able to resonate better with himself than with anything else.

There has now been research into affecting human biology over distance *and* time. In 1998, for instance, Dean Radin and colleagues reported distant effects in space (9,656km; 6,000 miles) and time (two months). In these experiments, ANS activity was collected from people in Las Vegas and successfully influenced in Brazil two months later.[18]

In a review paper titled 'Wellness Implications of Retroactive Intentional Influence: Exploring an outrageous hypothesis,' William Braud reported that for 19 experiments in retroactive intentional influence, the statistical 'p' value was 0.00000032, which is equivalent to odds against chance of around 3 million to one.[19]

In a 2001 study reported in the *British Medical Journal*, Leonard Leibovici reported that prayers from the present seemed to have affected the outcomes of 3,393 people with blood infections in the past.[20] The author, not believing that the results were possible, wrote that there must be something wrong with the way science was done if such a result were indeed true, because there were no methodological flaws in the research.

What is actually happening in these experiments? Looking at the traffic in Vienna experiment, did the influencers somehow alter the frequency of traffic entering the tunnel? At the time the data were collected, was a mental field exerting an influence on the traffic, or more specifically, on the drivers? Was information coming in from the future? Providing that no one had actually been counting traffic for another purpose, and therefore had knowledge of the volume of traffic at that time, did the influencers' minds actually influence the traffic flow? Or did the past just so happen to correlate with the present?

This might be the case. One hypothesis is that, just as there are probable future paths, so there might also be probable past paths – histories. A choice that we make in the present might select the appropriate history in the past. All paths, or histories, would lead to the present, just in different ways. With the Vienna research, then, we would simply have chosen a history where the frequency of traffic was consistent with the choices we were making in the present.

If you follow William Braud's 'outrageous hypothesis,' you might select better health today, and the seeds of that better health are then planted in your past (you correlate with that history). In the present moment you are still sick (although perhaps a little less sick), but the potential for health is now simmering inside you, and the future is set on a different trajectory.

WHAT'S THE POINT OF CHANGING THE PAST?

You might have spotted something in these experiments – that we only seem to be able to influence the past providing we don't know what happened. It seems a catch-22: we would only ever want to change stuff that we didn't like, but the fact that we don't like it means we know what happened, so we can't actually change it. Or can we?

If we do in fact influence ourselves, it raises the possibility of imagining offering comfort to ourselves in the past, perhaps when we felt lonely or afraid as children. I tried this once, when I thought back to the first time I remember feeling abandoned.

It was in the church car park in the summer of 1974. I was three years old, alone and scared. I thought my mum and older sister had gone home and forgotten about me, but they were just at the top of the stairs with a camera taking a photograph of me. I didn't realize this until years later, when I saw the photograph.

So I did a meditation. I imagined comforting my child self in the church car park in 1974, giving myself a hug and saying that everything was OK. I was like an angel to my child self. It's funny, but I felt a bit of an emotional release – relief of some sort.

Did I change my past? Perhaps, or perhaps I softened my memory of it. I wonder if there is a scale of influence. If we actually know what happened in the past, then maybe changing it takes more time and effort. It starts with a slight change in the memory and emotions associated with it. Then, as it changes further, we remember different aspects of it.

If the present is able to influence the past, then we're faced with another curious fact: the past isn't over yet!

Every moment in time, then – past, present, and future – is organic and in a constant state of change. The future isn't set in stone, and neither is the past. Life is neither mapped out ahead of us nor behind us. Our choices in the present moment have far greater potency to shape reality than we ever thought possible.

In the research into quantum physics we're going to look at soon, it does actually appear that the past correlates with choices we make in the present, which means there really are multiple pasts. I know – now things are just getting plain weird.

And what does that say about whether life is mapped out or not?!

KEY POINTS

- The mind is always interacting with reality.

- The past isn't set in stone. We are changing it via the decisions we make in the present.

- There are multiple probable pasts, just as there are multiple probable futures.

- The past isn't over yet – it is organic and changing.

LIFE EXPERIMENTS

- Meditate on a painful past experience, and imagine your present self moving back through time to offer comfort and support to your past self. Do you feel different afterward?

CHAPTER 7

WHEN THE CONDITIONS ARE RIPE

'When you expand your awareness, seemingly random events will be seen to fit into a larger purpose.'

DEEPAK CHOPRA

Before we proceed any further with how consciousness interacts with reality or how seemingly bendy time is, I feel that it's important to address a question that many people have. It's one that I have been asked on numerous occasions in different settings: why don't we see psi (intuition) effects every day, especially if the ability is such a fundamental part of who we are? Why aren't we clearly sensing the future every day of our lives?

What I've found is that, just as there are conditions under which we play better at sports or concentrate better on our work, so there are also conditions under which we experience more psi effects. If you really think about it, why wouldn't it be like that?

WHEN YOU'RE FEELING GOOD

I first began to think about ideal conditions when I was performing psi experiments of my own between 1994 and 1998. At the beginning of this period I was researching for my PhD in organic chemistry. I was building complex molecules in the lab that contained both organic units (carbon, hydrogen, nitrogen, and oxygen) and metals, and found that there were certain conditions under which the constructions worked better. For instance, if I removed all the oxygen from the flasks I was using, the experiments worked better. This was because the molecules I was building were so unstable that oxygen would break them down. But, unknown to my friends and colleagues (and even my housemates), I was performing hundreds of psi experiments in my bedroom at home and making similar observations about optimum conditions. Similarly, while I worked in the pharmaceutical industry developing drugs for cardiovascular disease and cancer, I spent numerous evenings conducting psi research in my living room, where I would attempt to guess the next color, suit, or card in a deck of playing cards, or influence the random sequence of the deck.

It became apparent to me that I got good scores when I'd had a good day in the lab, or when I was feeling particularly positive or confident, or when my belief in psi was high. But when I was feeling down, depressed (I had two bouts of depression, one in 1994 and the other in 1998), stressed, or even when I thought I wasn't any good at psi or was just wasting my time, I got low scores. When I was feeling like this I actually *expected* to score poorly and that is almost always what happened. When I averaged out all of my scores I was still on a small plus score, but when I examined only the times when I had felt good, I found my overall score was considerably better. This told me that there were definitely conditions that favored psi, just as there were definitely conditions that favored sticking atoms together in the lab at university.

What I found particularly fascinating was that when I was feeling down, sometimes my scores were very low (threes and fives out of 20) – so consistently low in fact that they were actually evidence of psi. Even when having a bad day you should still score around chance levels, but my scores on those days were much, much worse. I started to wonder whether at those times I actually was aware of the next card in a psi sense, but part of me, perhaps because I was feeling sorry for myself, was sabotaging myself, and so the low scores were indicative of my mind interacting with the experiment.

Eventually I would only 'play' when I felt confident, and therefore my scores were higher.

It would have been easy to just take an average of all the scores under all the conditions and just conclude that that was my psi score, and therefore my ability level. That's what we would normally do in science. But that would miss an important observation: that psi scores depend on emotional state.

Some might think of this as selective reporting, but actually it is quite pertinent to this kind of research – since we are researching a property of consciousness, surely the state of consciousness at the time should matter? That's a no-brainer if you really think about it.

My results echoed those of William Braud when he was working with the healer Matthew Manning. He noted that Manning's abilities seemed to vary with how he was feeling:

> The overall results for these 10 prerecorded EDA PK sessions did not differ significantly from chance. However, some interesting secondary evidence, that influences may have been occurring on a session-by-session basis (based on possible correspondences of session outcomes with observations of the influencer's changing motivations from session to session), was noted and described in the original report.[1]

IS PSI GENETIC?

I actually believe, as I discussed earlier with regard to presentiment, that the capacity for psi is innate. Presentiment is actually a type of psi. It is genetically wired into us to enable us to stretch our consciousness beyond seemingly everyday experiences. As we know, it would have saved our ancestors from danger, so nature would have selected those genes. And, just as with any gene, there will be multiple variants, known as polymorphs, of those genes. This means that different people will have different psi abilities.

A person's personal environment, diet, lifestyle, influences, education, etc., will also have an effect on the workings of their genes, as we know from our discussion of epigenetics earlier. It's no different from how some people have a specific variant of the oxytocin receptor gene that makes them more altruistic than most people, as I outlined in my book *Why Kindness Is Good for You*.[2]

So, rather than assuming that if psi were real we'd all be good at it, it's really just common sense that this wouldn't actually be the case. If presentiment and psi are indeed genetic, then we will definitely find some genetic variability, which could easily be tested experimentally.

In Schmidt's 1976 time-displaced paper, he pointed out that one person scored exceptionally high on several trials:

> *Particularly high PK [psychokinesis] scores on prerecorded targets resulted from a test by Dr. E.F. Kelly with Mr. Bill Delmore as subject, who had performed outstandingly in tests with several investigators.*[3]

The scientist Marilyn Schlitz, Ambassador for Creative Projects and Global Affairs at the Institute of Noetic Sciences, published research showing particularly high psi scores for artistically gifted people.[4] And in discussing presentiment research and much of his own, psychologist Dick Bierman said:

> *We're satisfied that people can sense the future before it happens. We'd now like to move on and see what kind of person is particularly good at it.*[5]

Once genes correlated with psi ability have been identified, I believe that a genetic test might actually show that some of the people most skeptical of psi research think that way partly because their life experience hasn't involved any episodes of it, and in turn that is because they have a genetic variant that predisposes them to be weak in this area.

As well as there being a genetic correlation, people undoubtedly block their own abilities because of a fear of social ridicule and even speak out against the phenomenon. I have worked with several people in science who secretly believe that there is something to it, even if they don't know what it is, but would never say so professionally or publicly.

For some people, accepting psi as real would force them to alter their worldview, and many people are just not prepared to do that, no matter how convincing the research. Others reject it on a purely scientific basis, believing that consciousness is inside the head, and so the whole field of research is flawed in some way, even though they don't know exactly how.

But, just as with any ability, if you believe you can do it, you tend to be better at it…

IF YOU BELIEVE

Belief can really make a difference. I used to be an athletics coach, and my success as a coach – all of my athletes were medallists at 'young athlete' or 'national junior league' level – came mostly because I helped the athletes to believe in themselves.

ESP experiments with believers and non-believers are referred to as 'sheep–goat experiments.' The sheep are believers and the goats are non-believers. The sheep do perform much better. A 1993 meta-analysis of sheep–goat experiments involving

685,000 guesses by 4,500 people gave odds against chance of 1 trillion to one.[6] Belief in ESP is definitely correlated with ESP ability, which demonstrates that ESP is real!

Hypnosis can be used as a technique to alter a person's beliefs about something. Interestingly, in an analysis of 25 studies involving hypnosis to amplify a belief in ESP, people scored higher under hypnosis than when they were in ordinary states of consciousness.[7]

A belief in psi certainly seems to be correlated with positive results – not just for the person being tested, but also the people conducting the study. Since the experiments are, after all, studying consciousness, it would be very surprising if the experimenters' consciousness didn't affect the outcome. To take an example, the head of PEAR research Robert Jahn and researcher Brenda Dunne wrote in a paper published in *Cellular and Molecular Biology*:

> *Another failed attempt at inter-laboratory replication involved a double-slit photon detector as a target. In this instance, the initial experiment was conducted by an optical physicist with a somewhat skeptical view of such anomalous phenomena, and produced only chance results. When his device was installed at the PEAR laboratory, however, significant extra-chance results were obtained following the same operational protocol.[8]*

In other words, an experiment run by a skeptic produced chance results and therefore no indication of psi, yet the same experiment run by believers in psi, and using the same equipment, yielded a positive psi result.

This type of phenomenon instantly poses a problem of replicability. Being able to replicate results in different labs is important in science. If a result can't be replicated then scientists usually assume that the original experiment was flawed. But with psi, this doesn't apply in the same way as it does for, say, the mixing of an acid and an alkali in different labs. When we are measuring consciousness rather than chemicals, the results in different labs will merely correlate with the beliefs of the people performing the experiments. In a real sense, results supporting psi only tend to come to those who believe in psi. This observation alone should tell us that psi is real.

DEFINITELY NOT RANDOM

Some people believe that it is normal to get positive results sometimes and negative results at other times. Together they will average out to zero, and so the positives and negatives are just random, and there is no evidence for psi.

Except that, first, they don't average out to zero. And second, even if they did, it wouldn't prove that what you were trying to measure was random – it would only show a *correlation* with randomness. It could well be that something else was varying and impacting the phenomenon you were trying to measure.

In other words, apparent randomness might actually be the statistical average of the conditions, or of how people felt during the experiment, and not actually an average of what was being measured. This would be particularly true if what was being measured was something displaying high sensitivity to the environment – like, say, consciousness.

To take an example, you could give a person a happiness score over a week that would be an average of their highs and lows throughout that time. But a person's happiness is very dependent on what's happening at the time, and the influences of other people. For many people, it would be their external environment and life situations that were varying and averaging out, not their innate happiness.

Remember that when I did my own psi experiments, my scores were very sensitive to how I was feeling, which in turn was down to what had happened in my life that day, so they reflected my environment and were not purely down to random fluctuations of psi ability.

EMOTIONAL CONNECTIONS

If we look at telepathy, around 70–80 percent of people have experienced some form of it.[9] In lab settings, however, the conditions are 'cold.' In being rigorous and eliminating external influences, experimenters often actually reduce the natural creative or emotionally connected space a person needs to be in to show telepathy. So, when results aren't positive, it may not be because the phenomenon isn't real but because the conditions aren't optimum.

Emotional connection can be particularly important. With the MRI and EEG studies outlined earlier, the experimenters purposefully chose people with emotional connections because they understood the importance of those connections. This was confirmed when the correlation between couples was clearly shown to weaken as their emotional connection decreased.

Why might this be? With telepathy, for instance, it's likely that the ability developed to serve an emotional or biological need (knowing when someone was sick, for instance), so we would expect it to be stronger where there was an emotional bond.

In his book *The Sense of Being Stared At*, Rupert Sheldrake described telepathy research that involved a mother and her mentally handicapped son with whom she had an extremely strong bond. The results were astonishing, with odds against chance of 10^{75} to one, which Sheldrake has pointed out is more than the number of protons in the universe.[10]

As discussed earlier, Sheldrake also reported that some dogs knew when their owners were coming home. This was also reflective of the emotional bond between the human and the dog.

After studying a large number of individual experiments, researchers Honorton and Ferrari wrote:

> *Four moderating variables appear to covary significantly with study outcome... Studies using subjects selected on the basis of prior testing performance show significantly larger effects than studies using unselected subjects.*[11]

In other words, people who have been shown to have more ability consistently score high, which may be innate or a product of believing in their abilities.

The second 'moderating variable' was:

> *Subjects tested individually by an experimenter show significantly larger effects than those tested in groups.*[12]

This would often have facilitated empathy, an emotional connection, which would have heightened the results.

The third was:

> *Studies in which subjects are given trial-by-trial or run-score feedback have significantly larger effects than those with delayed or no subject feedback.*[13]

This observation would have come about because getting positive feedback helps a person to believe in themselves, or their ability, and so they perform better. This is the case with almost any skill, innate or learned.

And the last was:

> *Studies with brief intervals between subjects' responses and target generation show significantly stronger effects than studies involving longer intervals.*[14]

This is basically just like optimum studying for exams. Brief rest periods work very well.

Pooling it all together:

> *The combined impact of these moderating variables appears to be very strong. Independently significant outcomes are observed in seven of the eight studies using selected subjects, who were tested individually and received trial-by-trial feedback.*[15]

******

So, what does all this mean in our lives? Quite simply it means that psi is real and your consciousness stretches out far beyond the inside of your head. It also suggests that all of the presentiment research and time-displaced research is real, and that the results are not random fluctuations of positives and negatives. So we can say with some certainty that the future impacts the present and the present impacts the past. Time is quite malleable, which suggests that life is both mapped out and it is not. This seeming contradiction is not a contradiction.

There are several futures ahead of us that are mapped out, but the thing is, we get to choose which one we experience. Therefore free will seems to reign supreme.

In the next chapter we'll clarify this further, looking at experiments using subatomic particles instead of humans...

KEY POINTS

- There are conditions under which psi effects are larger. This is common sense and is the case for almost any ability.

- A belief in psi influences psi ability. People who believe in it get better results.

- Researchers who don't believe in psi get negative results *because* they don't believe in it, which indicates its reality.

- Psi is stronger when there are emotional connections between people.

LIFE EXPERIMENTS

- As you go about your life, remind yourself that your consciousness is interacting with *everything* and that you have the ability to receive premonitions, presentiments, and precognitions. Keep a diary of any psi effects you observe in your life.

CHAPTER 8

QUANTUM INTERCONNECTIONS

'All human beings are interconnected, one with all other elements in creation.'

HENRY REED

Imagine you had a pair of subatomic particles and you sent one of them deep into space, to a galaxy about 100 million light years away. To give you some idea of how far this is, light travels about 300,000km (186,000 miles) in a second, so a light year is quite a distance.

But, here's the thing: if you were to stroke the particle in your hand, the one 100 million light years away would feel it **instantly**. Note that I said *instantly*. This is due to the entanglement mentioned earlier. Einstein had a bit of a problem with it because it violated the light-speed barrier that he laid down in his relativity theories. He called it 'spooky action at a distance' and believed that it wasn't possible. But the predictions have indeed now been confirmed.

Having one particle in your hand and the other in a distant galaxy is typical of what are called 'thought' experiments. They're pretty cheap to do! But in 1981 Alain Aspect and his colleagues at the Institute of Optics at the University of Paris at Orsay actually did send particles off in opposite directions.[1]

This was the first time the experiment had been performed. It was technically very difficult. The distance between the two particles was 13 meters (43 feet), and the results did demonstrate entanglement: when one particle was measured, the other one seemed to 'know.'

Physicists wondered if the strength of the connection would weaken with distance. So Nicolas Gisin and his coworkers at the University of Geneva, Switzerland, recently led another experiment.[2] The particles were separated by 11km (7 miles) this time – which is an astronomical distance for a subatomic particle. Relative to the size of the human body, it would be like a person traveling for around a million trillion miles, so the experiment was expected to give a fairly good estimate of whether distance mattered or not. And indeed it didn't. Measurement of one particle instantly impacted the state of the other, regardless of the distance separating them. The particles were said to be a 'single unified system.'

So far so good, but where things take a turn for the even stranger is that we can actually extend the idea of entanglement to the entire universe. Most physicists and cosmologists now agree that all particles were entangled at the beginning of the universe and therefore remain entangled today. What this means is that everything is interconnected in some way, even when it is not entirely obvious: you and me, a leaf on a tree in a distant forest, a grain of dust on the surface of the moon, a rock on one of Saturn's rings, and even a grain of dust in a distant nebula over a trillion kilometers away. We can think of the whole universe as a single organism.

In their book *The Non-Local Universe*, historian Robert Nadeau and physicist Menas Kafatos point out:

This suggests, however strange or bizarre it might seem, that all of physical reality is a single quantum system that responds together to further interactions. The quanta that make up our bodies could be as much a part of this unified system as the photons propagating in opposite directions in the Aspect and Gisin experiments. Thus nonlocality, or non-separability, in these experiments could translate into the much grander notion of nonlocality, or non-separability, as the factual condition in the entire universe.[3]

'Nonlocality' and 'non-separability' are technical terms for the fact that things are connected regardless of the distance between them.

Think about your relationship with the universe in the following way. As you think, you alter your brain chemistry. Thoughts and emotions shift neurotransmitters around in the brain. They also trigger chemical changes throughout the body. Try to recall a really embarrassing incident without your face heating up. As this occurs, the heat from your body is exchanging information with the atoms in your vicinity. As the particles in those atoms, as well as the ones that make up your brain and body chemistry, are entangled with those in the rest of the universe, the entire universe in some way feels the effects of your thinking.

It gets even weirder when you realize that with some types of particles (known as fermions and very numerous), no two can exist in the same state. Since there are unimaginable numbers of them spread throughout space (and inside everyone's body), the entire universe really has to *agree* with every thought you think in that their state must take yours into account.

But before we get a little too carried away with this idea, physicists have shown that even though particles are entangled, you can't actually send a message from one to the other. In that sense, there is no violation of Einstein's relativity.

Consciousness, on the other hand, *does* seem to be able to transmit meaningful information, which tells us that it is altogether different from subatomic particles and lends support to the idea that it is more fundamental to nature.

As for particles, given that they are connected over large distances, and distance and time are two sides of the same coin, does this mean that they are also connected across time?

SPOOKY ACTION BACKWARD IN TIME

Right at the heart of quantum physics is the famous 'double slit experiment.' This is where photons (particles of light) are fired at two slits in a piece of card to yield a pattern on a screen on the other side of the slits. It doesn't sound like the most fascinating experiment in the world, but it can demonstrate a phenomenon known as 'wave–particle duality' – that light can present itself as a wave or a particle.

It's all to do with how you do the experiment. If you set it up to measure particles you get a single mark on the screen, as if the protons were like bullets hitting the screen. If you repeat the experiment but this time switch the particle detector off, it turns out you get waves. You get a series of light and dark marks on the screen at the back, just like waves of water fanning out and overlapping with one another.

The key to the whole experiment, baffling as it is, is that you get either wave or particle behavior depending on how you choose to do the experiment, i.e. with the detector on or off.

So far so good! But here's where it gets a little spooky and begins to stretch the average scientist's understanding of the laws of physics. The experiment is typically set up from the start to measure either waves or particles. But what if you didn't decide which to measure until *after* the photons had gone through the slits?

It's an extremely technically demanding experiment, given that the photons are travelling at speeds of around 300,000 kilometers per second. You'd be in a bit of a rush to set things up after the photons had gone through the slits! But even if you could move lightning fast, as the photons had already gone through the slits, and therefore showed up as either waves or particles, it wouldn't matter how you chose to measure them. Would it?

You'd think! But it doesn't quite work like that. It turns out that how you choose to measure the photons *after* they've gone through the slits actually affects the way that they go through the slits *in the first place*. In other words, a choice made in the present affects how they behaved in the past. Sound familiar?

This is the essence of John Archibald Wheeler's famous 'delayed-choice experiment.'[4] Wheeler, who died in 2008 at the age of 96, was one of the world's most famous and influential scientists and made several hugely important contributions to physics. A long-time professor of theoretical physics at Princeton University, he also coined the term 'black hole' and taught students who have gone on to become some of the world's most influential physicists.

Wheeler's experiment was one of those inexpensive thought experiments, but Jean-François Roch and colleagues at the Ecole Normale Supérieure de Cachan in France actually carried it out and published their findings in 2007 in the premier journal *Science*, successfully showing this backward-time effect.[5]

For the techies reading this, here's the experiment they did. They used a beam splitter instead of slits and shot loads of photons at it. It's very common practice nowadays to use a beam splitter. It is typically a half-silvered mirror which lets half the photons through and deflects the other half along a specific path – off to the right, for instance.

The researchers placed a second beam splitter 50 meters (164 feet) away. It could be on or off, so that either waves or particles could be measured. Its purpose would be to join the two beams back together again (if it was switched on) or leave them be (if it was switched off). If it joined them back together again, they would see waves. If it let them be, they would see particles. But, as you will now suspect, they didn't make the choice whether to switch it on or off until *after* the photons had gone through the first beam splitter. They didn't have to move lighting fast either: they used a quantum random-number generator to make the choice at high speed.

The results proved that the choice made after the photons had gone through the first beam splitter actually determined the nature of the photons when they *reached* the first beam splitter. The 'delayed choice' determined whether they were waves or particles in the first place.

So, if you were a photon and you had the choice of which of two doors to go through, blue or red, I could show up half an hour *after* you'd gone through a door, and if I decided I wanted you to have gone through the blue door, then that's exactly what you would have done. From your perspective, my future choice would have affected your present choice. Your path would seemingly have been mapped out.

Weird, isn't it? But it's not really so different from the experiments where, for example, choices made in the present seemed to affect traffic volume through a tunnel in Vienna in the past.

The fact we're getting the same phenomenon showing up on two very different scales – subatomic particles and traffic flow

– tells us that it might really be how things work. Choices in the present are correlated with action in the past.

I'm using the term 'correlated' here because it is more accurate than 'determined' in that it suggests we're not actually impacting the past but just *selecting a different history* that correlates with our present-time choices.

ARE WE CREATING THE UNIVERSE FROM SCRATCH?

The delayed-choice experiment involved short timescales, but Wheeler actually scaled his thought experiment up to a cosmic level involving timescales of billions of years.

In this experiment, light is emitted from a distant quasar, a powerfully bright source of light at the center of a galaxy. As it travels toward us, it passes another galaxy. The galaxy's strong gravity acts a bit like a beam splitter in that it bends the light toward itself (it's known as a gravitational lens), but some light comes directly to us.

If we use a half-silvered mirror on Earth (a second beam splitter), then we can show that the light is coming to us as waves. (Remember, if we join the two beams together we're measuring waves.) If we don't use the mirror, we will see particles.

But the thing is, this time our delayed choice – whether or not to use the half-silvered mirror – is made billions of years after the light actually passed the galaxy. It's one thing to say that we're seemingly affecting the nature of photons a few millionths of a second ago; it's another thing to talk about affecting the nature of photons billions of years ago. But if we accept the findings of delayed-choice experiments, and that entanglement is unconcerned with distance and so should also be unconcerned with time, then a present-day choice should indeed force the light's path billions of years in the past.

As the science of quantum physics has shown us time and time again, counterintuitive predictions have a habit of turning out to be right when the experiments are actually done.

If we take the idea to its logical conclusion, what could the implications be? Could we even be creating the Big Bang – the birth of the universe – through the way we measure it today? Could we be selecting that particular history of the universe from multiple possibilities? Might there be other universes where the Big Bang wasn't how it all began? I personally don't know, but it's an interesting idea to explore if you want to stretch your mind a bit.

Wheeler's actual words were:

> We are participators in bringing into being not only the near and here but the far away and long ago. We are, in this sense, participators in bringing about something of the universe in the distant past.[6]

A valid way of thinking of Wheeler's experiment is that the light actually takes *all* paths in the first place. It is both a wave *and* a particle in two different realities, or histories. We just get what we measure. We're still acting backward in time, however, because we're choosing which of the paths the light takes in the first place.

This leads us to the conclusion that we have probable futures and probable pasts that we can choose from the point of power in the present. The question is, are the other paths always there and we're just not seeing them? Probably! These experiments would suggest that alternate histories *are* there, but we can only experience one of them – the one we measure (whether we use instruments or our five senses) – just as we can only get heads *or* tails on a coin toss and not both.

In a real sense, we don't actually change the past – ever – we just select different histories from the multiple different probabilities that are already there.

SUM OVER HISTORIES

Nobel Prize-winner Richard Feynman (a one-time student of Wheeler) developed a theory known as the sum over histories.[7] It is a mathematical thing.

It calculates the most likely path of a particle by assuming that it can follow every possible route (or history) to get from a to b. For instance, to go from one end of a room to the other, the particle would take all possible paths to get there, including flying around the world sideways or doing a little jiggle and then reaching the other side. Basically, anything is possible. The theory also allows for time-symmetry, the equivalence of moving forward and backward in time. It basically shows that any subatomic particle travels infinite paths through space and time, meaning that there are infinite histories for a particle at any one time. Could it be the same with our own pasts?

Revisiting the double slit experiment, Feynman suggested that the particle did actually take every possible path. Extending that to us, every possible history and future exists for us to select from. So any choice we make in the present is merely selecting the relevant history that reality took to get to us. Some, of course, are more likely than others.

Stephen Hawking and Leonard Mlodinow discussed Feynman's work in their book *The Grand Design*, writing, 'We create history by our observation, rather than history creating us.'[8]

ENTANGLEMENT IN TIME

As we have seen, the delayed-choice experiments show that particles can be linked not only in space but also in time. They are not classical entanglement experiments, because entanglement has historically described particles separated in space. In 2011, however, quantum physicists S. Jay Olson and Timothy Ralph showed mathematically that quantum particles could indeed be entangled across time, writing:

> *An intriguing property of the massless quantum vacuum state is that it contains entanglement between both spacelike and timelike separated regions of space-time.*[9]

This should come as no real surprise given that Einstein effectively fused space and time into the inseparable concept of spacetime. As Olson pointed out:

> *There really is no difference mathematically. Whatever you can do with ordinary entanglement, you should be able to do with timelike entanglement.*

In a groundbreaking 2012 experiment, scientists at the Institute for Quantum Optics and Quantum Information, in Vienna, Austria, led by Anton Zeilinger, did an actual entanglement in time experiment.[10]

The essence of the experiment was a little like the double slit experiment. The researchers basically showed that a choice whether or not to entangle two particles in the present determined whether the particles they were paired with were entangled in the past. Publishing in *Nature Physics*, the authors of the study described the phenomenon as 'quantum steering into the past.'[11]

A fascinating outcome of the experiment that will really stretch your mind (if it hasn't already been stretched enough) was that, due to the lifetime of particles, the choice in the present actually determined the nature of particles that no longer even existed. The state of their entire life had seemingly been determined after they had expired.

In the same vein as researchers into classical entanglement, these researchers pointed out that the particles were correlated in the present and past. That didn't necessarily mean that the present was causing the past, only that they were linked in that the past was *in relationship with* what was happening in the present. Again echoing classical entanglement findings, the researchers suggested that no meaningful information could actually be sent back in time. But the result confirmed again that a choice in the present selects the history that is correlated with it.

The scientists also made the point that the past only had meaning in relationship with the present. This echoes the sentiments of some spiritual teachings – that things exist only in relationship with other things. In other words, the past is not isolated and neither is the present, nor is the future for that matter, but all exist in relationship with one another. When one changes, the others change and correlate with it.

So, neither the past nor the future is set in stone. This is a very important point to understand. If you imagine life as a butterfly, the body is the present and the wings fanning out on both sides represent different futures and different pasts.

Once again we're led to the powerful realization that the point of power really is the present moment. Right now is where you get to choose your past and your future.

KEY POINTS

- Particles can be connected over huge distances and can be aware of each other's experiences. It's called entanglement.

- Entanglement classically describes inter-connectedness over distances, but experiments now show that it also occurs in time.

- Choices in the present affect the past.

- We could be creating the birth of the universe right now.

LIFE EXPERIMENTS

- Here's an idea to ponder. Since we're choosing histories and futures every moment, what if you chose to see someone in a different way? If you see someone as insignificant, for instance, you are following a trajectory into the future where they are indeed insignificant. What if you were to see them as confident and strong instead? Try it out and watch what happens!

CHAPTER 9

THE FABRIC OF REALITY

'As far as the laws of mathematics refer to reality, they are not certain, and as far as they are certain, they do not refer to reality.'

ALBERT EINSTEIN

Let's play with the idea of time a little more, not just because I find the subject incredibly fascinating, but because it's important for the overall question of whether life is mapped out or not.

If time is malleable and we can alter the future and the past, then it gives us the ability to change our apparent destiny. It suggests that, even if life is mapped out, we can change what's on the map.

Imagine the fabric of reality at the most basic level as an elastic sheet. Think of two points that are touching. Now imagine stretching the fabric until those two points are separated in space and time – they are no longer touching and it takes time to move between them. Try it with an elastic band – write your name on it then stretch it and watch the letters separate. At the most basic level things can be touching, but at the human level they are apparently separated.

Or imagine a drop of paint falling from the tip of a paintbrush toward a canvas. On the way down it splits into two drops, and they both land on the canvas at the same time but a few inches apart. Say the canvas represents your life from birth to death – from one side to the other – and the two drops represent you and a goal you want to achieve.

As time passes, you travel across the canvas and reach your goal. You got there using the three levels of creation. To you, that goal wasn't achieved until you made it happen. It didn't exist before that. But looking down from above the canvas, both droplets landed on the canvas at the same 'time.'

So now we have two different ways to think of time. There's the normal time that we experience on the canvas of life, where yesterday has already happened and tomorrow is ahead of us, but there's also the time from the perspective of above the canvas. Looking down on the canvas, two moments in human time can be seen at the same time. I'm suggesting that this perspective – out of time – is how it is at the level of the fabric of reality. I'm also suggesting that consciousness is integrated into reality at that level, so part of you has that perspective. I'll call that part 'Big You.' So one part of you sees life from 'canvas level' and another part, Big You, sees it from the fabric of reality, which you might think of as the inner canvas.

You and the realization of your goal started out as a single droplet of paint on Big You's canvas. You were connected (entangled in time, if we adapt the term), so on the canvas of ordinary life there would have been some form of magnetic attraction pulling you together through space and time. From your personal perspective, you sought to achieve the goal and did so. You 'attracted' it using the first two levels of creation. And yet from another perspective, as magnetic attraction is two-way, the goal attracted you. Information from the future came backward through time and influenced your decisions along the way so that you made the choices you needed to get there.

In this way, your future influences your choices in the present. You may think you are pursuing your dreams in life, but you are so connected to them that they, in effect, are pursuing you too. And this is where the third level of creation kicks in.

Another good way to picture this is that the future is a whirlpool up ahead on a river – it gently pulls you forward. Of course, this sounds as though life is totally mapped out. But, as you can now appreciate, you can choose to paddle in a different direction, with a new goal in mind. If you like where you feel you're heading then go with the flow, and if you don't like it then choose something else. As Ralph Waldo Emerson wrote, *'The only person you are destined to become is the person you decide to be.'* The power to choose is always yours. If you choose a new goal, you line up with a new whirlpool, a new future, and that pulls you forward instead. There is always a whirlpool up ahead; you just choose which one.

In mathematical and engineering terms, these whirlpools are 'attractors' – mathematical forms that things evolve toward. In life terms, we are the things evolving (or moving) toward the attractors.

Destiny really is pulling us forward in time. Much of that is because whirlpools are projected into the future by our hopes and dreams (even when they are mostly unconscious).

So you can say that choices in the present create what happens in the future, but you can also say that the future creates the present. And, if your mind isn't set for implosion yet, you can also say that they both happen 'at the same time.' It really all depends upon your perspective. It's all relative, as Einstein might have said.

HOW THE INNER AND OUTER ENVIRONMENTS CONNECT

Going back to the droplets of paint on Big You's canvas, you might think of the you on the physical canvas as the conscious mind and Big You as the unconscious mind, or something even deeper. You could call it 'higher self' or 'soul.' I am using the term 'Big You' because I don't want to exclude anyone who may feel uncomfortable with the spiritual or religious associations of those terms.

You and Big You, the conscious and unconscious minds, are connected. A well-known metaphor is the iceberg. The conscious mind represents the tip of the iceberg, the small part above the water, and the unconscious mind is the larger part underneath the water that we're mostly not aware of. Without the unconscious mind, we wouldn't be able to function. It maintains the beating of the heart and the functions of all of our internal organs.

The unconscious mind is actually very *much* conscious; it's only seemingly unconscious to us because it's out of our normal range, so to speak. Arguably, it is far *more* conscious than the conscious mind.

So, life as we know it is only part of the picture. A much bigger part of us is portrayed on a very different canvas. Or you may like to think of it the other way around. Think of Big You as having a 'you' on the canvas of the physical world. You could think of yourself as its fingertip, making a print on a canvas that contains a nice picture of planet Earth. You are a physical extension of Big You – a portion of your consciousness that is experiencing life in the physical world.

SHINING SOME LIGHT ON COINCIDENCES

This idea can help us shine some light on coincidences. Almost all of us have experienced coincidences in life. Some people brush them away, while others see a deeper meaning in them and label them as synchronicities – meaningful coincidences – a term coined by Carl Jung when describing clusters of seeming coincidences.

A typical argument against coincidences is that they are just clusters of random events and therefore have no meaning at all. For instance, if you flip a coin you don't get heads then tails then heads then tails again, but clusters of heads and clusters of tails that do average out to around 50:50. This is absolutely true. And some events most likely do show up as clusters in life. But this doesn't prove that all coincidental events are random clusters, only that some *could* be.

I'd say that many coincidences are meaningful. They reflect a connection between people and events and are often a consequence of us using the three levels of creation.

For example, a conversation with a friend, Mike, in a café about an idea you have for a book could lead to Mike arranging to meet his friend Julie, who has another friend, Amy, who is in publishing. Mike meets Julie in the same café because he likes it there and is hoping that he can arrange an introduction to Amy.

Julie quite likes the café – it's her first time there – so she arranges to meet Amy there the next morning. She doesn't tell Amy on the phone about Mike wanting an introduction. Amy arrives the next morning, but Julie calls her on her cell phone to say something's come up and she can't make it. Amy decides to stay anyway and have a coffee. It's a nice café!

You happen to be there too, because you use the café as your office. You're at the next table and end up striking up a conversation. It turns out that Amy is the perfect person to help you. You have a book, she's in publishing! Wow! What a coincidence. You were just talking about your goal with your friend Mike yesterday. Synchronicity! Spooky! Or so it seems.

We could easily explain it away as a random cluster of happenings, where you and Amy just happen to be in the same place at the same time. But in doing that we would miss the fact that the meeting actually happened because information travelled through a social network (according to the second level of creation).

It is certainly not random, even though it could be explained like that when we only look at the end result. Many events in life cluster like this because of information travelling through our social networks. Conversations between people introduce different odds over random things happening. To explain them away as random only shows that we haven't understood how the connections occurred.

Let's look at coincidences from a deeper perspective, from the third level of creation. Your desire to have your book published would have connected you and Amy on the inner canvas. So now, going back to our elastic sheet metaphor and stretching the sheet up to the physical level, you and Amy are seemingly not connected. You don't know each other, nor have you met yet. That deeper connection isn't immediately obvious, but nevertheless it is exerting an effect. The fact that you are connected introduces a kind of magnetic attraction, and so the people and events come together in time and space. It's seemingly random, but it certainly is not.

I'm not ruling out that some coincidences may be random of course, although fewer, I'd suggest, than we think. There are far more connections in the world, in both space and time, than we are aware of. There are wonderful mysteries to be unravelled around us. I think it's quite exciting.

So here's how I think we create coincidences in our lives. Having a thought about something – say, a goal – drops the idea into the unconscious mind and connects us to our goal on that level. The drops of paint fall onto the physical canvas, and we are drawn toward our goal. Some events might happen *en route* coincidentally, but others will occur because the intention and the goal are connected.

Our minds are as connected to the entire universe as leaves are to trees. We just don't notice because we have convinced ourselves that consciousness is a product of brain chemistry, and so we filter out much of the magic and meaning in the world.

Elizabeth and I were in New York City a few years ago. I had been speaking at a conference, and we took a few days' holiday afterward to check out the city. Elizabeth had recently written a humorous book called *God Must Be a Man* and said she'd love to hand it to Joan Rivers to see if she liked it. About an hour later, we had got lost in the city and just decided to walk down a particular street. As we were walking by an apartment building, a large car pulled up right beside us. Who stepped out of it? You guessed it: Joan Rivers!

A few years before that we had been on a flight from Spokane, Washington, to Los Angeles, California, and Elizabeth had been flicking through the in-flight magazine when she had found a feature on Dominic Keating, the English actor who played Malcolm Reed in *Star Trek* (the series set before the time of Captain Kirk). She showed me the story and said she'd seen him on the front cover of *Hello* magazine a few months earlier and had wanted to write to him for advice because he was a British actor based in LA, but she didn't know how to get in touch. As an actress herself, she also wanted to make the transition from the UK to acting roles in the USA, and she thought that Dominic Keating seemed like a really nice person. She said the feature had reminded her that she wanted to get in contact with him, so she'd try to find a way.

How's your presentiment? I think you are already guessing what's coming. We were staying in Los Angeles with our good friend Olivia Bareham. She happened to be friends with LeVar Burton (who played Geordi La Forge in *Star Trek* and also Kunta Kinte in the award-winning drama *Roots*). I am a huge fan of *Star Trek*, so a couple of days after we arrived, LeVar invited us, through Olivia, to watch an episode that he was directing.

We drove to Paramount Studios and arrived at the set. Who was filming the scene we got to watch? Yes, Dominic Keating. And even better, being a nice guy, he came over and said hello. When he learned that Elizabeth was an actress looking to get some opportunities, he gave her his cell phone number and offered to help in any way he could. He even made a few calls, set her up with some important meetings with potential agents and managers, and called her a few times over the next couple of weeks to see how things had gone.

Random? Absolutely not!

ARE OUR THOUGHTS DESTINED?

If we're so connected to this inner canvas, or psychological field, you must be wondering if all of your conscious thoughts emerge from there. And if so, are all of your thoughts predestined?

First, I'd say that, so long as we feel we have some control over our lives and experience the consequences of our actions, it doesn't actually matter. It's just a philosophical argument.

But, side-stepping that point for the moment, I'd personally say that it's a two-way street. Everything in life and nature is two-way. Plants impact the environment by giving off oxygen and fertilize the soil when they decay, and in turn the environment nourishes the plant. We breathe in air and breathe carbon dioxide out. There's push and pull, give and take, to everything.

I'd suggest that it works the same with the conscious and unconscious minds – between the physical canvas and the inner canvas.

How does it work? The thought of attaining a goal seeps into the unconscious mind, so you and the attainment of the goal become connected on that level. Then, just as the thought of making toast eventually leads to a slice of toast, eventually the goal emerges as fulfilled in your everyday life.

Of course, you don't just close your eyes and it miraculously appears in front of you. It would be handy if things worked that way. Mind you, maybe it wouldn't be such a great idea if it happened that fast. Judging by the fearful and stressful thoughts that many of us have, I shudder to think of what we might manifest around ourselves. Thank goodness there's a bit of a time-lag. Just as an artist takes time to fill in a sketch when creating a painting, so we have to give our goals a bit more focus – to be sure we're clear on what we want. The actual physical process of attaining goals occurs through the first two levels of creation, but the connection is established through the third.

And in two-way fashion, information from the inner canvas colors your thinking through the connection between your conscious and unconscious minds. And so it influences some of your choices and intuitions so that you are drawn to people and places that you are connected to on that inner level.

So we create our personal realities using our free will, but some of the choices we make have a deeper meaning that we might not realize at the time. There is both free will *and* destiny.

In the next chapter, we'll look at just how we create events in the world.

KEY POINTS

- There are two ways to look at time – from on the canvas and from above the canvas.

- The conscious mind experiences everyday life, but the unconscious mind (Big You) is on the higher level.

- Events are connected at this level. The present creates the future, the future creates the present, *and* they both create each other. They are all connected, or correlated.

- Coincidences happen because people and events are connected.

LIFE EXPERIMENTS

- Every time a coincidence happens, reflect on the idea that there are deeper connections in life.

- Think of your goals and aspirations as events to which you are already connected. They are already attracting you, so trust that every decision and action that you take is the right one.

- Meditate on the idea that you are part of the fabric of reality, and that part of you always occupies that inner space. Take note of the inspirations you receive from that level.

- If you are correlated with someone close to you, be an angel in their life by correlating with who you would both be if they were living their dreams.

CHAPTER 10

MIND INTO MATTER

**'Consciousness creates all, or all that
we know reflects the particularized
creations of consciousness.'**

ROBERT BUTTS

Now that we are starting to understand some of the connections
in our lives, we can explore how mind *becomes* matter.

Let's continue with the assumption that consciousness makes
up the basic fabric of reality, so that, rather than thinking of the
fabric as a quantum field, as we might do in physics, we think of
it as a field of consciousness.

Things obviously appear spaced out in the world – you and I are
clearly not holding hands right now – but, as we go deeper and
deeper into the field, the seeming divisions between everyday
things fade away to nothing. You can look at a tree and think of
it as physically separate from yourself, but if you were to peer
inside the atoms in your body, or the atoms that made up the
trunk of the tree, you would eventually arrive at the same place

and reach the profound realization that there *is* no separation between you.

The deeper we go, the more connected we become, until we reach the level of reality where we are just different expressions of the same thing – just as in physics, subatomic particles are thought of as different expressions of the quantum field.

You could imagine that thoughts and intentions at this level of reality produce waves, just as spoken words produce sound waves. You could think of them as waves of consciousness. But, just as with the photons in the double slit experiment, I would like to suggest that thoughts and intentions are also particles.

Let's play with the idea that intentions produce particles of consciousness. So, just as different types of quark (elementary particles that don't have any known smaller bits) combine to form protons (specifically, a proton is composed of two 'up' quarks and a 'down' quark), particles of consciousness might combine in some way to form quarks.

If you think of it in this way, subatomic particles – protons, electrons, quarks, and others – are actually made of consciousness.

We don't usually think of consciousness as a physical substance, and of course there might not be any actual particles of consciousness, just thoughts that form fields that create structure – just as sound can create form in, say, sand if you place the sand on top of a speaker. But, staying with the particle idea for now, in the same way that clouds of cosmic dust coalesce into planets, so consciousness may coalesce into all of the physical things in our world.

Following this through, the entire world therefore has consciousness – not just the plants and animals, but the rocks, clouds, oceans, dust, and even the air we breathe. Clearly it's a different type of consciousness from the one we share, but it's consciousness just the same. I'm not suggesting that an atom makes decisions to hang around to watch *Star Trek,* or enjoys going to the gym, but that it has some awareness, however rudimentary it might be to you and me. I'd say that a biological neural net is required for our type of self-aware consciousness. But that doesn't preclude a background 'hum' of consciousness all around us.

The entire world is alive then, from the smallest atoms to the largest stars, and our collective unconscious thoughts and beliefs must produce the waves and particles that form this physical world that we all share. Since the conscious mind is focused on the everyday world, this is obviously done out of conscious awareness, and that's why we don't typically bend and lift objects by thought alone. Collectively, however, we do so much more without even realizing: together, we create the world.

The fact that the unconscious mind is focused on the inner world is why we get a degree of permanency in the world – rocks, trees, and physical landscapes – and things don't just appear and disappear into thin air with every thought the average person thinks.

In fact, it's quite handy that there is a division between the conscious and unconscious minds. The unconscious mind, focused inward, maintains the fluid construction of the world, while the conscious mind, focused outward, experiences it.

So the world is a mental construction. The everyday, seemingly solid world is a projection from the field of consciousness, like a cinematic projection onto a screen. Our intentions and our hopes and dreams create much of our reality according to the three levels of creation, but ultimately it boils down to the impressions we make on the reel.

In a real way, just as water fills the shape of a cup, so our life events reflect the 'shape' of our mind – its intentions, beliefs, emotions, ideas, hopes, dreams, loves, fears, and judgments. It's not an exact fit – of course there are forces that influence us, and some events just happen, although we probably do have an unconscious awareness of their likelihood. Still, it leads to the intriguing question: was the universe created by a thought?

THE BIG THOUGHT

It is well established that the universe began with the Big Bang. The main view is that this was a random fluctuation in the quantum field – a random ripple, or wiggle, in the fabric of reality.

Many people take the view that this does away with the need for God. Certainly, if we think of creation as a random wiggle, then there is no actual *need* for God. But there's no proof that the wiggle *was* random. My contention is that there was a conscious act of thought that *caused* the wiggle and set in motion all the physical laws.

Think of the birth of a baby. If we just did the math, the baby would appear at birth. One moment it didn't exist, and the next moment it did. Zero (no baby) becomes one (a baby) – seemingly a random fluctuation. There's no need to conclude that anything came before the baby. But that's only because we are ignoring the actual mechanics of where the baby came from. In reality we know that there is a lot more to the process than birth.

What about the birth of the universe? Current thinking reduces what might be quite a complex and beautiful process of creation down to nothing becomes something, zero becomes one. That's mostly because we can't probe the depths of the fabric of reality with current technology, and all we're left with is mathematics. That is a beautiful and elegant language (it's one of my favorite subjects), but it reduces many things to zeros and ones – at least until a more elegant formula is worked out. And I personally feel that on those grounds, it's incorrect to assume that no God exists, and especially to state it as fact.

WHO OR WHAT IS GOD?

So how might God fit into this picture? I would like to explain my idea of God, as it may differ from yours.

My view of God is very different from the classical impression of a white-bearded man sitting on a cloud answering our prayers and passing judgment on us. In my opinion, some of the religious rules around the world are not as relevant today as they were when they were first written, thousands of years ago. I believe that it is the presence of these seemingly unbendable rules, along with the rigid idea of the white-bearded man, that actually create much of the atheism we see in the world today. People naturally move to the other side, so to speak, when they hear ideas and rules that sound restrictive or unintelligent.

I'd say that the main elements of religion are the important things – love, empathy, compassion, forgiveness, respect, and kindness. These are universal to almost all the world's religious and spiritual traditions. But, sticking with the idea of God for the moment, although the white-bearded guy is an outdated concept in most intelligent people's minds, it doesn't mean that God doesn't exist.

My contention is that we are all God. God is merely the innermost portion of ourselves.

Why?

GOD

If we accept that the fabric of reality is infinite – which we have to do if we acknowledge that the universe that emerges from it is infinite – we can also say that consciousness is infinite.

To me, God *is* that infinite consciousness, and you and I are particularizations of it, just as classical elementary particles are thought of as particularizations of the quantum field. Indeed, Einstein said that,

> We may therefore regard matter as being constituted by the regions of space in which the field is extremely intense.

We are, in a sense, parts of the field of God where consciousness is intense, or focused. We are like protons in the quantum field of God.

As particles are formed from units of consciousness, so we emerge *out of* God. Each of us, technically speaking, is the body of God, enabling God to experience life in each of our individual ways. God *is* the Father (and Mother) in that sense – not just the Father of the occasional spiritual teacher throughout history, but yours and mine as well. Many people like to think of God as a parent, looking after us, loving us and serving us; someone we can talk to at any time. I like that idea myself. It's comforting in that way. Maybe it's because it's the only way our minds can really perceive God.

Imagining God as a person (of sorts) makes me think of God's humanity. If love forms the foundations for human life then it has to come from somewhere – and where else but from God? So I think of God as love, and therefore, as God is infinite, God's love is infinite too.

With this in mind, I don't believe that God ever takes sides. Many wars have been fought with each side believing that God was exclusive to them. But the sun shines equally on everyone, and God's love shines equally too.

So, no matter where I might hide or what I feel I might have done, God's love will always know where I am and shine on me. My job really is just to notice that and pay it forward by loving others too. Sometimes it's so comforting just to know that there's someone, or something, out there with your best interests at heart.

I hope that no one is offended by this way of looking at God. This is merely my preferred way of understanding life, and I'm not suggesting that we all suddenly become religious zealots. But I would ask atheists, in the spirit of compassion, to permit each person the freedom of their own beliefs because, after all, atheism is a belief in itself because there is no scientific proof of its assertions.

SAYING A PRAYER

So how does this view of God tally up with our relationship with God? What about saying prayers?

The majority of people in the world pray, albeit in different ways and to different ideas of God. We assume that God is selective in answering prayers because sometimes the prayers seem to be answered and other times they don't. I know some people who are always debating in their own minds whether God exists at all, and when they feel their prayers have been answered they are believers, but when they feel they have prayed really hard and their prayers haven't been answered, their belief wavers. Some actually conclude that they are unworthy of having their prayers answered or that they don't deserve to be happy.

In the spirit of the information presented so far in this book, I would like to suggest that it is *our* job to create our lives, and we shouldn't wait around hoping God will do it for us. God may be the field, but we shape the field. When we create using the three levels of creation, we are shaping the body of God. We are the sculptors of reality.

It can be extremely satisfying to know that we have that freedom. It instantly removes the belief that we are unworthy of the life we want. That's merely what it is, after all – a belief. It isn't reality, but a belief *about* reality.

When we feel empowered in this way, *that* is the power of God, because we are consciously using the power of God to create.

This doesn't mean that we shouldn't pray, though. Prayer can still be a way of accessing help. There's more than one way to do it.

SOME DIFFERENT WAYS TO PRAY

Asking God to make something happen for you, which is what a lot of people do in prayer – certainly almost everyone I know – is a negative presupposition. This means that it presupposes that you have no power to make it happen yourself. You're surrendering your own power in your own mind, rendering yourself impotent. What you're really stating is that you are powerless to create, so you need to ask God to do it for you.

It's like a negative placebo effect (the nocebo effect). This is where you develop symptoms of illness because you believe you have the illness, even when you don't. Your belief in your own powerlessness can therefore be reflected in what you create around yourself using the three levels of creation. You might find there are people in your life who make you feel weak, and situations in which you appear to have little or no control. You might even find that you appear to be stuck in situations. You miss creative solutions because of your belief in your own powerlessness. You simply wait in the hope that God will say 'yes' this time. But you do have the power!

Ask for Help

A much more powerful prayer is to ask God to *help you* create what you want. That way you still ask for help, but you're also positively affirming that you have the power to make it happen. You're just asking for a wee bit of inspiration.

Trust

Another way to pray is to trust God; to trust that everything will work out for your highest good, given that love is the essence of reality.

A friend of mine once sent me one of those circular e-mails that fly around the world several times. I couldn't find its source, but I am grateful to whoever started it because I found it meaningful. It said that God only ever answered prayers in one of three ways:

1. Yes.
2. Not yet.
3. I have something better in mind.

If you trust that this is true, you can stop stressing about things and go with the flow in a relaxed way. You have a new creative thought in your mind: *Things will work out for the best for me.* I have to say that I've used this affirmation since I was a child, when I first heard my mum say it. Her father (my papa) would always say it to her, and it gave her comfort during a long period of post-natal depression.

This thought simply creates what is best in your life, unimpeded by stress, worry, and fear about the consequences of not getting what you want.

Be Grateful

Last but not least, as they say, is a prayer of gratitude. It is a prayer that says, 'I love what is showing up in my life now,' or 'Thank you, God, for all that I have and all that I am.' From this space, we notice good things all around us. Happiness increases, personal energy increases, and we are better able to point our minds toward the good things that we desire. And, as we notice good things, so our focus helps us to create more good things, which we are then grateful for – and we have a virtuous circle.

GOD'S WILL VS OUR WILL

It is a deep cultural belief held by many that everything that happens is God's will. How does this fit in with our ability to create our lives?

Before I go any further on that point, I'd like to reiterate that I am only presenting my own perspective, my own beliefs, and I hope that my ideas are not in any way offensive to anyone.

I'd say that since we are God, then technically our will is God's will. As I pointed out in the last chapter, there is two-way communication between the unconscious and conscious minds. We make decisions and create what we want, and we also receive some flashes of inspiration to help us meet with the people and situations to which we're connected. Since God is the infinite consciousness of the field, then effectively there's a two-way communication between us and God. We ask, and then we receive a hint, a hunch, a feeling about the right way to go forward. In this sense then, God never forces us to obey, but only ever offers us the assistance we ask for.

I think we also have to consider that there is an overall direction to life which forms a background, underlying, force of destiny. It's like a gentle current on a river that we hardly notice, so that we seem to have complete control over where we are paddling to, but eventually we do end up going where the current takes us.

I think such a current flows through all of our lives and goes largely unnoticed. Broadly speaking, I think it is a current of love. That view comes from the observation that evolution has written into our DNA genes for cooperation and love that have glued our societies together and basically insured the survival of our species. It also comes from an intuition. That love is a force of destiny feels like the truth to me.

Of course it's easy to say that evolution is random, and that cooperation developed as a survival technique. That is the mainstream view of evolution, and I can see the logic in it. It makes sense. But given what I've presented so far, I am led to the conclusion that there is a predestined direction to evolution.

Does this mean that evolution is driven by the will of God? Perhaps, but in the day-to-day workings of our lives, we are only influenced by this in the broadest possible sense. In fact, I think of God's will as more of God's *influence*. We eventually evolve to love one another but we are free to get there in our own way. It's always up to us.

When we surrender to the influence – or spirit – of God, we align ourselves completely with love. We see God in everything, and because that is what we are focusing on, we create love, beauty, and perfection everywhere we go. This is the path taken by all great spiritual masters.

In this state, it feels as though we are doing God's will, and in a sense we are, but it's actually our own will. So surrendering to God doesn't mean giving up free will, just being inspired to use that free will to create go(o)d things.

KEY POINTS

- Physical reality condenses out of the fabric of reality.

- Atoms and subatomic particles are alive.

- We are God and God is us.

- There are different ways to pray.

- Our will is God's will.

LIFE EXPERIMENTS

- Meditate on the thought that all of reality is conscious, and that your mind is your tool for aligning with it. Take a walk in nature, and try to sense the consciousness of different forms of life – trees, animals, plants, flowers, etc.

- Remember that you have the power of the universe at your fingertips. It flows through you. Whatever you create, create it with kindness.

CHAPTER 11

LIFE BEFORE LIFE AND LIFE AFTER DEATH

'Consciousness is the basis of all life and the field of all possibilities. Its nature is to expand and unfold its full potential. The impulse to evolve is thus inherent in the very nature of life.'

MAHARISHI MAHESH YOGI

I'd like to move away from the discussion about God now because I'm aware that while some people are passionate believers in God, the religious connotations do not appeal to everyone. So I'll continue in this chapter from a neutral perspective and leave you to make your own mind up.

Let's pick up again on the idea that Big You is out of time. If this is the case then technically it existed before you were born and will still be there after you pass away. It can see both ends of the canvas of your life. What might this mean?

PRE-INCARNATION

You are living a life here on Earth, and you don't know anything else. Big You, however, has a wider perspective and can make a brush stroke anywhere. Where to make the stroke?

Do you think your birth was a random flick of paint on the canvas? Or could you be part of a bigger picture? Could Big You have decided to paint the canvas at a particular place, in a particular environment, with a particular climate of personalities and probable influences?

What would you do if you were Big You? Of course, technically you *are* Big You, and therefore you might want to make sure that everything is right for you. Given that we tend to check out stuff before we buy, could it be that Big You would do the same? Might Big You check out the environment and climate on the canvas before parachuting into it, so to speak?

Say you personally had the option to enter a new world. Would you want to choose where, how, and when you planned to settle? Would you check out the climate and the socioeconomic conditions? Would you look up a few reviews from people who had already been there? Would you want to pick some conditions that resonated with you?

I think most of us would. I would, anyway! So, if you accept that you do exist outside of time, then it's likely that you had a hand in choosing, say, your birth date and time, where you were born, your family environment, the conditions in the area at the time, even your most probable school, even though you have no memory of all this and might even look around you and say, 'There's no way I would choose this! And him? Why would I choose to have him in my life?'

From the grander perspective of Big You, there will be a reason. If Big You can see the whole canvas, including the other personalities in the vicinity of where it's thinking about setting up camp for 90 years or so, it will be able to see your most likely influences up ahead, for the first few years at least. It's similar to how you could look down on some little ants from above and see the terrain ahead of them.

THE TREE OF PROBABLE LIFE

So, from the beginning of the planned lifetime, Big You will be able to see a map of the life before you. It will be able to see the most likely influences on you, and also the most likely forks in the road. But we know that you have free will, so could Big You be looking at more than one map?

The choices Big You sees are 'probable' choices that you could make, where each junction branches out into two probable futures. Big You can see the future of both choices.

I like to use the metaphor of a tree to explain this. Life starts with your birth at the base of the tree. As you tend not to have too many choices in early life because your parents are making them for you, your life is like the trunk of the tree, heading in a set direction. But as you start to make your own choices, the tree begins to grow branches that represent the probable futures that each choice would bring. And along each branch there are more choices, which produce more branches, and so on. I call this the 'tree of probable life.' It maps out the most probable paths that your life could take.

So, instead of having a single destiny – a specific path that your life is supposed to take – there are several possibilities. Many of them will, of course, arrive at the same place (or just about) – as the French poet Jean de La Fontaine wrote, 'A person often meets his destiny on the road he took to avoid it' – but they will get there in different ways. These places will be the intentions, or the hopes and dreams, of Big You, but the probable branches permit you the free will to choose for yourself.

I sometimes wonder why so much of nature has the same appearance, from trees to blood vessels (look at the blood vessels in your eye) to river deltas, and many other forms in nature. Perhaps the growth rules of trees, blood vessels, and rivers reflect the nature and growth of consciousness – and that there is always free choice within growth.

WHY DID I COME HERE?

So let's home in on some actual reasons that Big You might have had for starting your life the way it did. As an example, let's say you wanted to work on developing the tone of your leg muscles. You decided to go somewhere for a week to do it. Would you choose to visit a flat place or a hilly place? Chances are you'd go for the hilly place because that would help you to develop your muscle tone.

If you wanted to develop more positivity, on the other hand, even amid challenges, would you go to a place where everyone was happy, or would you try out one where you would be likely to come across some strong-willed, negative people? Or would you go for something in between? Maybe you've faced this kind of challenge already and would prefer to relax! The point is that you have options.

I'd say that a property of consciousness is that it seeks to expand, and that's why the universe is expanding. For us, evolution lies in the expansion of our consciousness, ultimately in moving from self-preservation and selfishness to recognizing our interdependence and treating each other with love and empathy. In this way, we are all evolving. And Big You is also evolving. Your evolution is its evolution.

There are many directions in which we can expand, or evolve, in consciousness. Let's say Big You wanted to develop the ability to be peaceful and in control when challenged. In this instance you might be born into a large family where there was always a lot of noise, or be drawn to friends whose behavior was random and chaotic. In these situations, patience would be a real challenge, and finding time to be still wouldn't be quite so easy. You would need to be extra focused to find peace. You would have to stretch yourself. But you would get there in the end – you would expand your ability to find peace amid chaos. You might not expand *much* at first, but the experiences might set the tone for other phases of your life.

With this simple idea in mind, you can look at your life challenges not as burdens – which we all do at times – but as opportunities to take yourself to new heights.

ALWAYS AN OPPORTUNITY

I'd like to share with you a personal example which illustrates that difficult situations can present us with opportunities for expansion.

Personally, I thought that I was good at being peaceful, even when challenged. Since leaving the pharmaceutical industry I had read a lot of books, been to several talks and seminars, and practiced meditation on a regular basis. I was actually quite proud of myself.

At least that was until I took a job as a college lecturer while I was writing my first book. One class of 16-year-old boys was so challenging that I let them out 45 minutes early in our first three-hour mathematics class because I couldn't cope. To give you an idea of the situation, let's just say that they told me very clearly what I could do with my decimals. I got in my car, drove around the corner and cried.

Within the first 10 minutes of that class, all the strategies that I'd learned about being calm and positive had gone right out of the window. On my way home I decided that my health was more important than the job, and that I would go into work the next day and tell the head of department that I wasn't teaching that class any more. If she had a problem with that, then I was resigning my post.

The next day my plans were thwarted because the department head wasn't in. I told my colleague, Ian Anton, about the class and he laughed, which wasn't quite the kind of empathetic reaction I was hoping for. He quickly pointed out that my experience wasn't all that unique. He explained to me that the kids could smell my fear and would take advantage of it because they could tell that they were the alpha males and not me. He compassionately explained that I was entitled not to take the class, but that it would be better for me in the long term if I did. It was great advice.

I spent the weekend working on my self-development. I did visualizations around courage and confidence. I repeated affirmations. But I also reminded myself that I had a chance to make a real difference to these boys' lives as well as learn to be a better teacher than I'd been before. Fueled by that attitude, I went back to that class. I dealt with the characters with humor, empathy, and kindness, but I also commanded respect. It went really well, for the boys and for me.

By the end of the course I felt like Robin Williams' character in the film *Dead Poets Society*. I had a queue of 16-year-old boys waiting to shake my hand, including a dyslexic boy who had never passed an exam in his life but was now beaming with pride at the 'A' he had obtained. Some said they felt that they had learned more on that 12-week course than in all their previous school years.

I had learned a lot too. I had grown in confidence and learned not to run away but to face challenges head on. I now had the actual experience of how well that could work out.

In terms of my tree of probable life, both branches existed. I could have chosen to walk away, and that would have been OK. I'm sure I'd have been challenged somewhere else along the way! Choosing to continue with the class wasn't an easy option – make no mistake, it was painful at first – but maybe having painful experiences is important for our personal growth and fulfilment. Maybe for many people it is an inevitable part of growth. Look at your own life. Have you grown as the result of your challenges? We don't become experienced in life by reading books and going to talks. We learn from them, but it is in the *application* of what we learn that we gain experience and wisdom.

We don't always grow from our challenges, of course – or at least not noticeably – and things don't always work out. I have had personal experience of that too. With some stuff in my life I'm still wondering what the point was. Things can sometimes be too overwhelming. Sometimes walking away is the most appropriate thing to do. That might have been the point – learning to have the courage to say 'Enough is enough.' One way or another, everything that happens to us can be an opportunity for growth.

YOU... AND YOU... AND YOU

I've spoken a lot so far about you and Big You, but you know it's not just about you, it's about all of us. Your family members, friends, coworkers, others in your social circle and beyond all interact with you and they all have their own journeys to make through life. They are also evolving through their own trees of probable life and have Big selves working out where their branches overlap with yours and how growth can be mutual.

With this in mind, some people like to think of life as a play with many different characters, some of whom are on our stage for a 'reason, a season or a lifetime,' as they say. We are the characters, and we set the stage before making our entrance. We have a script to follow, but it is only a draft. We have choices about how we want to interpret it, and we can improvise if necessary.

We may be playing one particular character now, but how many parts might we have played?

HAVE I BEEN HERE BEFORE?

Would we be able to grow more if we were part of a few different paintings on the canvas, or a few different plays, or... lifetimes?

Think about it. The evolutionary history of our species is a big stage. Imagine the dramatic opportunities!

As humans, we like to do lots of things and have lots of experiences. We grow through each of them. Maybe this reflects an aspect of Big You as well. Big You might also be having lots of experiences, or, from your perspective, living different lives, each with a tree of probable life. From your position on the canvas, these might be in the past or in the future. So, since you are part of Big You, you could think of them as past or future lives.

Let's return to the droplets of paint on the canvas. This time, don't think of them as you and a goal you want to realize, but as different lives that Big You is experiencing. The canvas now represents the entire canvas of past and future human evolution.

Some droplets might land in places of war and others in times of peace. Some might be male and some female. Some might find themselves in a world of riches and others a world of poverty. Some might be primitive, others advanced. Some might be in warm climates and others in cold. There are different colors of paint too. There is a vast number of possible experiences to be had.

And here's the thing: Big You might experience these lives simultaneously, or even in a different kind of time that we're not able to conceive of, but as far as you are concerned, each droplet is independent, separate from the others in space and time.

As we are all connected to the Big versions of ourselves, and get a sense of its reality from time to time, this may be where the fascination with past lives comes from. The concept has been part of many spiritual and wisdom traditions around the world and throughout history. In science, no one can say that there are no past lives. The idea is 'unfalsifiable' in that it can't be proven wrong, but that doesn't make it false.

Also interesting is that many of Big You's experiences are technically in your future. That may well explain premonitions. Prophets have been around from biblical times and before, and I believe that their visions were of future lives. But, since life evolves along trees of probable life, not all of their visions occurred along our present branch of the tree. They might have seen what was most probable at their time in history, but clearly we have made some different choices along the way.

Coming back to choice, and remembering that we can change the future and the past, might we be able to change our future lives and our past ones as well? Wow! Am I stretching things a bit too far?

Think of it as Big You having its own tree of probable life. Why not? Surely it has choices too. Just as you select different histories and futures in your own life according to your choices in the present, so Big You may select different histories or futures in terms of lifetimes. And those lifetimes will correlate with who you are now and the choices that you are presently making.

The psychiatrist Brian Weiss is famous for taking people under hypnosis into a past life. Past-life regression therapy is a very popular technique that is used by many psychiatrists and psychologists today.

Weiss has experimented with future-life progression too, and interestingly, one of his findings has been that when a person resolves an emotional issue in the present, their future life changes as well. Or, in the terms I have been using, they are correlated with a different branch on their Big Self's probable tree of life and therefore have a different growth trajectory.

The reason for Big You's multiple lives is likely to be just the same as our reasons for multiple experiences – to grow. This can be growth in creativity, intellect, physical capabilities, compassion, you name it, and can come in any one of an infinite number of ways. Does it also carry on into infinity?

You might wonder if there is an end point, an ultimate destiny for you and Big You.

IS THERE A DESTIN(Y)ATION?

On your canvas, the end point is the end of your life. That's one way to think about destiny. I'm not sure there's any way around that. All rivers lead to the sea, as they say. How you get there, though, is largely up to you. You might glide in gracefully, happily reflecting on your life experiences, or you might skid in sideways with a huge grin on your face and say, 'Wow! What a rush!' We're all unique.

And then what? Off into another life? Is there ever an end point of physical existence? I can imagine that there is. It's when there's nothing more that can challenge you. You are whole, complete. You see everything for what it really is. Your whole existence is to teach and serve. You leave then and move on to a new canvas of experience of consciousness, a completely different kind of playground, so to speak.

Perhaps, in the grander scheme of things, just as every particle emerges from the quantum field and returns to the field and all biological life exists on the Earth but returns to it, so all of life emerges from the fabric of reality and eventually returns to it.

What about Big You? If the overall evolutionary process is toward love, you could say that its destin(y)ation will be expanded consciousness, which, as we have already seen, is associated with a sense of love and interconnectedness with all life. Perhaps the ultimate expanded consciousness, and hence destiny, is conscious fusion with infinite consciousness, or God, if you prefer.

IS THERE ANY EVIDENCE FOR LIFE AFTER DEATH?

Is there any evidence for life after death that might lend support to what I've discussed so far?

Some of the best evidence comes from people who have had a near-death experience (NDE), where they were brought back from the brink of death and remember what happened to them while they were being resuscitated and the ECG was flatlining. There is a mainstream view that these experiences are hallucinations caused by the brain being starved of oxygen, but I'd say that many of them are actually evidence that life continues after death.

NDEs are a lot more common than you might think. Millions of people around the world have had them. In a Gallup poll during the eighties, for instance, around 1 in 20 Americans reported that they had had one.[1]

A landmark study by Dutch cardiologist Pim van Lommel, which was published in 2001 in the medical journal *The Lancet,* followed 344 consecutive cardiac patients who had been successfully resuscitated following a cardiac arrest. Sixty-two of them (18 percent) had had a near-death experience.[2]

In a 2011 paper published in the *Annals of the New York Academy of Sciences*, van Lommel wrote:

> *Because the publication of several prospective studies on near-death experience (NDE) in survivors of cardiac arrest*

have shown strikingly similar results and conclusions, the phenomenon of the NDE can no longer be scientifically ignored. The NDE is an authentic experience that cannot be simply reduced to imagination, fear of death, hallucination, psychosis, the use of drugs, or oxygen deficiency.[3]

He went on to challenge the mainstream view of consciousness as a side effect of brain chemistry as too limited to explain the phenomenon:

The current materialistic view of the relationship between consciousness and the brain, as held by most physicians, philosophers, and psychologists, seems to be too restricted for a proper understanding of this phenomenon. There are good reasons to assume that our consciousness, with the continuous experience of self, does not always coincide with the functioning of our brain: enhanced or nonlocal consciousness, with unaltered self-identity, apparently can be experienced independently from the lifeless body. People are convinced that the self they experienced during their NDE is a reality and not an illusion.[4]

One woman told me of an experience that her mother had had as a 10-year-old child. She said she could:

...vividly describe the [hospital] procedure – what she saw, what was going on and what she heard. She described the tubes and the red blood going into a jar and the people in the room. She said she was watching

it up on the ceiling, out of her body. She seemed quite
calm, just observing it all.

Looking down on a scene like this is called veridical perception.
Another woman told me it had happened to her mother too:

She was a young woman undergoing a major operation
to remove a piece of bone from her hip to replace the
bone that had become diseased on her spine. She
had had TB in the lung when she was 14 years old and
although she did recuperate, it reappeared a few years
later and was eroding the bones in her spine. It was the
first operation of its kind in Scotland [1954/5].

The nerve pain was excruciating. During this long
procedure she said that she was suddenly aware that
she was floating above the operating table and could
overhear the conversation below. She had no pain and
was aware of a light. She felt drawn to the light and
was not unduly concerned that she had apparently left
her body. Then she was aware of coming round after
the operation.

There are various reported degrees of NDE, ranging from leaving
the body to going into a light and coming out on the 'other side.'
Many people accurately describe the resuscitation procedure, as
well as the conversations between the medical staff.

Dr. Michael Sabom once did an experiment involving 32 people
who had had NDEs.[5] He asked them to describe the resuscitation
procedure that was performed on them. All of them reported it

accurately, with no major errors. He also asked 25 quite medically knowledgeable people to describe the resuscitation process, but 23 of them made major errors in their descriptions. The people who had had NDEs really had been watching from above.

Some 'NDEers' reportedly have the experience of passing through a tunnel before appearing on the other side. Some are met by relatives and loved ones who died years before. Many people also report being met by an intelligent light source that they describe as an angel or a religious figure.

In the book *Dying to Be Me*, Anita Moorjani recounted her near-death experience and her memories of the other side.[6] She explained that she felt connected to everything and everyone.

What if, rather than dismissing these accounts as lack of oxygen to the brain, or even fantasy, we take many of them as showing us something about reality and listen to some of the lessons these people have shared with us? What are these lessons?

Many NDEers emphasize that our thoughts, words, and actions have consequences, even when we don't immediately see them. The most important thing they repeatedly tell us is how powerful love can be. In fact, the point of life, they say, is to love.

An NDE often completely changes the person who has it. In van Lommel's study, patients were interviewed after their resuscitation, then again after another two years and again after eight years. For most, the experience had a lasting positive effect. They tended to show their feelings more, to be more accepting of others, to be more loving and empathic, to have a greater involvement in family life, to have a greater sense of the meaning of life, a greater interest in spirituality, and a greater appreciation of ordinary things. They also had much less fear of death and a greater belief in the afterlife than before. Clearly they had evolved in consciousness.

This is hard for the mainstream scientific community to accept. As we know, the traditional view of consciousness is that it is a product of chemicals in the brain, so it exists only when the brain is alive. Once the brain flatlines, according to this view, there can be no conscious experiences.

But with the advent of powerful new brain-imaging techniques, our understanding of the brain is beginning to shift. We are learning that, rather than our thoughts being caused by brain chemistry, much of what happens in the brain is caused by what we're thinking about. It's not just a one-way street where chemicals produce thoughts and emotions. For example, fMRI brain imaging shows that some areas of the brain light up when we think of a certain thing. There's even talk of reading people's minds by noting which areas of the brain light up when they think particular thoughts.

Technology is now being developed to help people with locked-in syndrome to communicate, to enable paralyzed people to move prosthetic limbs, and even to assist Professor Stephen Hawking, whose motor neuron disease is eroding his ability to communicate.

For many people, the latest research into the brain hasn't established that consciousness can exist outside the brain, but

NDE research suggests that this is the case. When the brain dies, consciousness can no longer be 'received' by the brain and the five senses, but it still perceives things outside the body. This is how many NDEers are able to watch over their resuscitation procedures.

WHISPERS FROM THE OTHER SIDE

If we exist on the other side after we die, it doesn't take much of a stretch of the imagination to assume that there are other 'people' – spirits, beings, angels – there too. NDEers tell us there are, and opinion polls show that the vast majority of people believe in their existence.

In the book *Destiny of Souls*, counselling psychologist Dr. Michael Newton relates the hypnotic regressions of many of his patients, and they describe, with astonishing similarity, the nature of the 'spirit world' and the reality of 'life' for the souls who live there.[7]

There is no definitive scientific proof of this, as we can't physically measure any of it. To the average scientific mind it probably sounds preposterous. But how can we know? All we're left with is what we ultimately believe – what feels right to us individually.

I personally believe that we have spirit guides – beings who are focused on the inner, shared landscape and therefore don't have a foothold on physical reality, but who help us. I also believe that deceased relatives sometimes visit us and under certain conditions it is possible to see them. About 20 years ago both my mum's deceased parents visited her, one night after the other.

My gran, who had died a few years earlier, looked as real as a person. My papa, who came the next night, looked more like a photographic negative, as he was semi-transparent.

My friend Kyle Gray, the Angel Whisperer, has been able to see 'dead' people ever since he was a small child. Though it was a bit strange at first, it's just so normal for him now that he hardly gives it a thought when someone appears in front of him.

I once went to a seminar by the psychic medium Gordon Smith, whose accuracy in relaying information from people's deceased relatives was absolutely astounding. One girl's brother 'came through' and Gordon suddenly found himself humming a tune and then making rap movements with his hands and arms. It turned out that the song was the brother's favorite, and it was a rap song.

Gordon's abilities have been scientifically investigated. Professor Archie Roy, Emeritus Professor of Astronomy at Glasgow University, wrote: 'Gordon Smith provides names, addresses, events, and descriptions sharply relevant to a person's life and the lives of those they have known.'[8]

I believe that we are occasionally reminded of our hopes and dreams by our spirit guides, and probably also by our deceased relatives. I have always felt that my papa is watching over me. Although it might sound daft to the scientific mind, I take comfort in communicating with him in my mind's eye, and I believe that he helps me when I ask. Sometimes I get a clear picture in my mind, or a feeling or inspiration about something, and even though he passed over in 1982, I believe this is his way of impressing the answers upon me.

Spirit guides do the same thing. Some mediums get even clearer messages, often hearing an actual voice or physically seeing their guides and having conversations with them. It's also very common for people to see deceased loved ones a day or two before their own death. Many nurses have seen them too, although few publicly admit it.

Of course, it's unlikely that deceased relatives, spirit guides, and angels just sit around on clouds all day waiting to communicate with us. As spiritual leaders tell us, heaven is not a physical place where we hang around for eternity. Pope John Paul II pointed out that heaven is a state of mind. It's a space of consciousness. Back to consciousness again!

BORN WITH A SENSE OF DESTINY

The first thought to enter my head after I have learned something fascinating has nearly always been *How can I explain that?* This started when I was very young, and now it is actually my job to explain stuff. It's an odd way to describe being a writer, I suppose, but I feel that's exactly what I'm doing through my books and seminars – explaining how things work.

When Elizabeth was 11 years old she had the overwhelming sense that she was to be an actress. It changed her life. Ever since that day her life has been focused on acting.

Where did these ideas come from? It's easy to say that the people around us, TV, and our environment subconsciously give us suggestions. I absolutely believe that too. It's common sense. We take on board all kinds of suggestions without even realizing. In fact, my best ever card trick was where I seeded the idea of a particular card several times throughout an evening with friends. I had taken that card out of the deck earlier and stuck it to the underside of the table. I then asked one of my friends to mentally pick a card and tell us what he'd chosen. There was a fair chance he'd choose the card that I'd 'suggested,' and he did. I then took the deck, slammed it down on the table and asked him to pick out his card. Of course, it wasn't there. So I joked that I bet it had gone right through. We all looked under the table (a few glasses of wine had been involved by this point) and there was his card. To say that everyone was stunned would be an understatement.

I did a similar trick at a family gathering for my dad's 60th birthday, but this time I stuck the card to the outside of the window. After someone had 'chosen' the card, I threw the deck at the glass. Family members were shocked when they saw that the card was left stuck to the window, but not half as shocked as when they went to remove it and found that it was on the other side. One of my aunts got really spooked after that and gave me funny looks for a year or two afterward.

Many of our ideas are seeded by our environment, but I think it would be wrong to conclude that *every* instinctual sense comes to us that way. As we have seen, there are three paths of intuition. Auditory and visual cues (people, TV, environment) only account for one of them. I'd now add a fourth, which is that we receive information, impressions, impulses from our Big selves, who, of course, set the overall direction of our lives in the first place. I'd say that this is why many people feel they have a sense of purpose, a destiny, even though they can't explain it.

It's also why we can meet people for the first time and feel as though we've known them all our life. If our Big selves communed above the canvas and decided to overlap or intertwine branches of their trees of probable life, we may feel some form of faint recognition on the canvas when our paths cross. This could be dismissed as just gelling with people we have things in common with, but sometimes we have nothing in common with the people we recognize, and it would be wrong to conclude that this was the only reason for the mutual understanding.

Many people don't feel they have a sense of purpose at all, and I suspect that there's a reason for that too. Maybe it's best they don't know, at least for now anyway. That way they can carve out their own path, which might be the whole point for them.

I sometimes picture having a sense of destiny as having a tiny map in your mind that guides you along the roads in life – a satellite navigation device that reminds you to 'turn left at the next junction' – although it speaks through intuition or presentiment and not in an annoying voice. It's an inner knowing of where you're going and what you need to do to get there.

I felt this very strongly in 1998 and 1999 when I was working in the pharmaceutical industry. The sense that I was supposed to be writing books and teaching seminars was becoming so strong that at times it was all I could think of. I knew that I just *had* to do it, even though the thought of leaving my job terrified me at first, and the idea of speaking in front of people was also pretty scary.

But we always have free will. The map doesn't force us to do anything. It's just a guide, just as a street map is a guide. A street map might make it obvious which would be the best street to go down, but it doesn't force us to go down it. We can always choose the other probabilities on the tree of probable life.

SOULMATES

Let's now consider the concept of soulmates, which I'll bet you're all wondering about now – the idea that there's one special soul out there for each of us.

Imagine you and another soul form a relationship, for whatever reason. That relationship might be a romantic one, or it might be friendship, or familial, or even something else. Whatever the reason for it, let's suppose for now that Big You and Big Mr (or Ms) Right decide that they want to spend time together in human life. So, to use our metaphor of paint droplets, they leave the paintbrush together and separate on the descent to the canvas, landing clearly separated in space and time. One is born before the other, and they are not initially in physical contact with each other. But, according to the commitment they made before they were born on Earth, there is a connection between them. It's as if they are entangled. Here's where I think it gets fascinating.

As they are entangled, what happens to one, even though they are unaware of it, is correlated with what happens to the other. Wherever one goes, whatever experiences they have, the other's behaviors and experiences will somehow correlate with it, even though they might not have 'met' yet. So when they do finally meet, or get together if they already know each other, they will be a perfect fit. There is a familiarity there, a connection that feels right, even if it initially appears all wrong.

Have you ever become friends with someone and it just so happens that you've had similar histories? Friends can be soulmates, too, although to distinguish this from the romantic idea we might perhaps refer to them as 'soul buddies' or, as my old friend Kenny used to say, 'bro.'

Sometimes a soulmate can be someone who pushes all your buttons – and I'm not speaking in the physical sense. I laughed out loud when I heard Wayne Dyer say that he once wrote a magazine article called 'Your Soulmate is the Person You Can't Stand.' Your soulmate might easily be someone you *never* want to be with in the romantic sense, but by continually pushing your buttons they will help you to expand, to turn into the person you need to become for some other phase of your life. That might be the whole point.

Clearly there is an element of life being mapped out going on here. I'd bet that if a relationship or friendship was important, it would take place regardless of which branch your tree of probable life unfolded along. In other words, regardless of which choices you made in life, the other soul's choices would correlate so that there would always be a high probability that you would meet and form a relationship. If you were getting to the meeting-point earlier, then obstacles would get in your way to slow you down, and if you were moving too slowly then seemingly miraculous coincidences would occur to move you along a bit. Phew! I'll bet if you're single you're thinking you can relax now.

Immersed in this material while I was writing this chapter, I had a vivid dream one morning where I was the same age as I am now (41) and was jogging with some friends, one of whom I recognized from university. I was ahead of them, so I stopped in a pub to take a short rest. I met Elizabeth in there. She looked different in the dream. Her hair was shorter, she was dressed differently, and she had some kind of tattoo, but she had the same personality as she has now. I was instantly attracted to her. When I woke up I felt that this was another branch of our respective trees of probable life. Our meeting was always on the cards.

So I believe that there are such things as soulmates, even though I was playfully scoffed at the first time I raised the subject in a science lab. Whether all soulmates have the same sort of connection, or whether there are different reasons for their relationship, I don't know for sure, but the idea makes a lot of sense to me.

We certainly live in an interconnected world where reality is shared. In the next chapter I'd like to discuss collective forces of destiny, and how we as individuals fit into it.

KEY POINTS

- We exist for a reason. It's about growth.

- We evolve along a tree of probable life where our choices lead to probable futures. Big You experiences both.

- There is scientific evidence of life after death.

- You have been here before (or at least Big You has).

- Big You evolves through you.

- Some people are born with a sense of purpose, like an internal map or sat nav.

- Soulmates are Big selves who agree to become entangled on Earth, being drawn together through time and space to meet each other.

LIFE EXPERIMENTS

- Look at your own life. Have you grown from many of your challenges?

- Do you feel you have a sense of purpose or destiny? What is it? If you don't, meditate regularly with the intention of finding deeper meaning in your life.

CHAPTER 12

COLLECTIVE DESTINY – WHERE YOU GO, WE GO

'The interdependency of humankind, the relevance of relationship, the sacredness of creation is ancient, ancient wisdom.'

REBECCA ADAMSON

So, now that we've considered destiny from an individual perspective, what about from a collective one? We all live in this world together, after all. Do our collective hopes and dreams draw us to a collective reality? Is destiny mapped out for humanity, or are we making it all up as we go along?

In purely cosmic terms, there is an ultimate destiny for us. The sun will go supernova in about 5 billion years (give or take a day or two), so the Earth will be pretty much toast. Although, who knows what stage of evolution – spiritual and technological – we'll be at by then? We might have no need for the Earth at all, having long since moved on.

Aside from this, and the chances of an asteroid slamming into us in the next 100 years or so, or a CME ripping our atmosphere off, I'd like to address how our collective destiny relates to the choices we make.

I believe that the cosmos does exert a major influence over us. I started out with chronobiology in this book to put across the point that we are not separate from the cosmos. Its rhythms and cycles are so etched into our genetic make-up that what it does, we do too, just on a different scale.

We have looked at the cycles of the Earth, sun, and moon, but I believe that there are other cycles – larger ones – that impact us too. As to the exact mechanism, though, I can only speculate.

Much has been written about December 21, 2012, the end date of the Mayan long count calendar. Some people believe that it marks the end of the world or the beginning of the end of the world. I do not believe that for a second. The Mayans merely marked out cosmic cycles and built their calendars around them. In some ways, the end of their long count is no different from the end of a century or a millennium for us. Although the Mayans were marking real cosmic cycles and not just an arbitrary period of, say, 100 or 1,000 years as we do. It's not the end, just the flipping over into another period. For them, December 21, 2012, marked the end of a cycle with a unique alignment of planets and stars.

I think the ends of cycles and beginnings of new ones mark new beginnings in our individual and collective psyches. At the turn of the year, for example, many of us write down our resolutions for the new year. I have a little ritual that I follow every year, and it really does impact the way my year unfolds. Some time between Christmas and New Year I make a trip to the shops to buy a new notebook that I will use to write down the many different thoughts, inspirations, and ideas I will have throughout the year, and I buy a new diary to list my speaking events and meetings. I take great care in getting just the right notebook and diary. I search for ones that feel right, whether that's due to the color, texture, size, or something else. Then, on December 31, I summarize my past year, looking at how I fared and comparing that to the aspirations I had, and I write out my new goals. The whole thing is highly symbolic of a new start for me. I get really excited after Christmas because I can feel the new start coming, and I'm deciding how I want the next yearly cycle to go. Loads of people do a similar thing.

In the book *Choice Point*, which I cowrote with Harry Massey, producer of the film of the same name, we discussed the nature of cosmic cycles and how they might affect us.[1] We suggested that when one significant cycle ended and a new one began, there was a short span of time in between where crises often occurred. These times are windows of opportunity, or 'choice points,' where our choices have the greatest potency to affect how life unfolds in the next cycle.

As I am writing in 2012 there seems to be a great many crises in the world, from political upheavals and financial crises to crises of overpopulation, fuel, poverty, food, and climate change. Could it be in some way related to the end of the cosmic cycle marked by the Mayan calendar? I suspect it is.

Whether this is due to a biological impact or a symbolic one is open to debate. I think it's actually a bit of both.

To take the symbolic idea a little farther, did you know that more people are admitted to hospital due to traffic accidents on Friday 13th than at any other times of the year? A doctor told me that, but it's also backed up by research. In a paper published in the *British Medical Journal* in 1993, for instance, researchers showed that, even though there were far fewer vehicles on the M25 motorway around London on Friday 13th (presumably many superstitious people stayed at home), admissions to hospital from traffic accidents were 52 percent higher than on Friday 6th.[2]

Conducting a much wider study, a team of scientists from the University of Oulu in Finland, publishing in the *American Journal of Psychiatry* in 2002, compared the deaths from traffic accidents on Friday 13th in a national population with deaths from traffic accidents on other Fridays of the year.[3] They found that more people died in traffic accidents on Friday 13th than on any other Friday. Interestingly, the increase was mostly in women (maybe they're more superstitious), and 38 percent of deaths involving women on Friday 13th were concluded as being a result of Friday 13th itself, as there was no difference in female deaths on any other Friday, but a large peak on Friday 13th.

The authors believed that this might have been due to the anxiety generated by the Friday 13th superstition, something known as paraskevidekatriaphobia. Bet you can't say that! Actually, I once said the word at the start of a public talk to around 100 people and jokingly added, 'I'll give £5 to anyone who can repeat that word back to me.' A guy named Steve in the front row immediately said it back, and I had to give him the £5! The word derives from the Greek words *paraskevi* (Friday), *dekatreis* (13) and *phobos* (phobia). Friday 13th anxiety is also known as triskaidekaphobia and even friggatriskaidekaphobia (Frigga is the Norse goddess after whom Friday is named).

So, the effects of Friday 13th are not due to some dark force that makes us crash our cars, but to fear itself. It's the belief that Friday 13th is unlucky for some that causes accidents. It's all in the mind.

This doesn't mean we should dismiss it, though. The placebo effect is all in the mind too, and we can't dismiss that. The effects of Friday 13th are real for some people, just as the placebo effect is real and the subsequent chemical changes in the brain and body are real. In terms of Friday 13th, it's the individual and collective expectation of problems that results in problems.

The expectation of great changes at the end of great cycles is also in our collective psyche, or at least in enough people's psyches to effect great change. So global and personal crises seemingly happen *to* us, but many could in fact be created *within* us.

So, there was always a high probability of global (and personal) crises a few years either side of December 21, 2012, and our Big selves would undoubtedly have seen them coming. They would have been on the collective probable tree of life, as well as our individual ones in the great orchard of probable trees of life.

MENTAL AND EMOTIONAL CLIMATES

What other collective forces could be around and within us, steering us along particular mass trajectories?

Mass emotion can also act like a force upon us. I like to think of our mood as our mental and emotional climate, which I picture as a little cloud above our heads. A person feeling happy might have a brightly colored cloud, and a person feeling gloomy might have a gray cloud. I think it was years of watching cartoons as a child (and as an adult) that gave me the idea.

Our emotions often drive what we create in our lives. In one study that examined old college yearbook photos, researchers were able to correlate a person's career earnings with their smile in the yearbook photos from two decades earlier.[4] People showing a genuine smile, known as a D-smile, which is indicative of happiness, were much more successful throughout their lives than people whose yearbook photos showed them making an ordinary smile.

It happens on a mass scale too. Just as clouds in the sky mix and merge, so do our mental and emotional clouds. Researchers Nicholas Christakis and James Fowler showed that happiness and depression were contagious. Studying a social network of around 12,000 people, they showed that being happy made surrounding people happier, and the same was true for depression.[5] Our cloud, in other words, colors other people's clouds. I discussed this research, as well as explaining how emotions actually infect people and therefore how to protect yourself from negative emotions, in my book *The Contagious Power of Thinking*.

However you like to think of it, we are all connected. Each person's emotional climate ripples, not only through their social networks, but also through the deeper fabric of reality, like a pebble dropped in a pond. It mixes and merges with the waves created by everyone else, and sets up mass waves that ripple across the metaphorical pond.

So, we share a collective mental and emotional climate that represents the average mental and emotional state of humanity. And, just as a person's mental and emotional climate influences the nature of their life, so our collective mental and emotional climate influences what we create on a global scale.

The same kind of thing happens on the in-between levels – in homes, workplaces, towns, cities, countries, and continents – and as we are all a part of these climates, where they go, we go too. So, rather than always being in control of our mental and emotional state, sometimes we are quite significantly influenced by the climate around us, on both a local and a mass scale. The challenge for us is to gain control of our emotions, which we can do by becoming more aware of our own minds. Meditation is a useful tool for this.

BE A GOOD EXAMPLE

Many people are willing to accept that we create events that mirror our collective mental and emotional climate. That's all well and good. But what about wars?

Often the product of belief and human emotion, conflicts and wars in the world reflect conflicts and disharmony in our collective hearts and minds. Anger, hatred, fear, or a sense of injustice are the food that nourishes wars.

I hope you're now beginning to realize that the solution to war really does start inside each of us. If mental and emotional climates can create war then they can also establish peace. During a recent visit to Ireland, Aung San Suu Kyi said, *'Peace is not the absence of war around us, but the absence of war within us.'*[6]

The Chinese philosopher Lao Tzu said:

> *If there is to be peace in the world, there must be peace between nations.*
>
> *If there is to be peace between nations, there must be peace between cities.*
>
> *If there is to be peace between cities, there must be peace between neighbors.*
>
> *If there is to be peace between neighbors, there must be peace in the home.*
>
> *If there is to be peace in the home, there must be peace in the heart.*[7]

And if you flip it round, you can see the link going the other way: peace in the heart leads to peace in the world. There really can be lasting peace in the world when there's a large enough mass of people with peace in their hearts.

Most people can relate to this in some way, as it makes sense when we just look at our own lives and how we infect others with our emotions; people around us infect us too. In fact, so obvious is this to the average person that when I first published *The Contagious Power of Thinking*, the most common feedback I received was that what I wrote about was 'startlingly obvious.'

It's also obvious that most people really hate war and want peace in the world. Numerous people even attend antiwar demonstrations, such is the intensity of their sentiment. Many of them protest very angrily, and I can say that honestly because I have attended such a demonstration in the past and seen many very angry people there.

Angrily protesting does bring attention to the issue of war, so it does a lot of good in that sense, but in another way it actually fuels the climate of war because anger and hatred are what many protesters are holding in their own hearts, but just pointed in a different direction to those actually involved in the war. Every angry thought sends a vibration through the web that joins with similar thoughts, and eventually, a 'hatred cloud' begins to form in the collective psyche. I would suggest that when it reaches a certain intensity it arrives at a tipping point, and that's when conflict breaks out somewhere in the world, perhaps where there is a weakness or where conditions are ripe.

Similarly, then, love in our hearts and minds can create a climate that promotes cooperation, tolerance, and kindness.

After declining to attend numerous antiwar demonstrations, Mother Teresa said, *'As soon as you have a pro-peace rally, I'll be there.'*

Changing the world, as Gandhi and many other luminaries have repeatedly told us, starts with ourselves. Look at yourself, then, completely honestly, and decide if what you are projecting outward is consistent with what you want to see in the world. If it is, then good! Continue to be an example to others. Help them to get there too. If it is not, then make the necessary changes within yourself so that you are sending out the right waves, so to speak.

Mother Teresa offered some powerful advice on this, saying, 'What can you do to promote world peace? Go home and love your family.'

MASS CURRENTS

Let's now pick up on the idea that Big You and, collectively, Big Us would have seen things coming on a collective scale. Our Big selves would have been able to see the ebb and flow of human experience over the canvas, and each of us would have entered at this point with an awareness of the probability of having to face crises. In fact, we may have helped, through our own choices and emotions, to bring about the very crises we now face.

We are part of a collective current. If this collective current is flowing toward peace, cooperation, empathy, and kindness, then developing the necessary knowledge and skills for finding these qualities in our own hearts will be part of our inner destiny. We will be guided toward making the right decisions. If the wrong people happen to be in power then they will lose that power, and people who can make an enlightened difference will take their places.

If the collective current is flowing toward disaster, however, we will be guided toward making the errors of judgment that ensure that happens, whether that's through selfishness, short-sightedness, a love of power, or some other reason. Our inner purpose will then be concerned with how we deal with the situation; how we get through it, and who we can become in the midst of the great challenges it presents to us.

But whatever the current when we were born, it might have changed direction several times since then, as we have made personal and collective choices. I believe that each of us holds enormous power to affect the mass current by the choices that we make today. We all have free will. The question is: how do we use our free will to shape our lives?

I touched on the subject earlier when I described the three levels of creation, but in the next chapter I've distilled most of what I've ever learned that can help you to create what you want in life.

KEY POINTS

- Change usually comes at the end of a cycle, which is part cosmic and part symbolic.

- We have our individual mental and emotional climates, but we are also part of local and mass mental and emotional climates.

- Mental and emotional climates influence the nature of events in our individual lives and in the world.

- We change the world by changing ourselves.

- Peace in the world begins with peace in the heart.

LIFE EXPERIMENTS

- Pay attention to your own mental and emotional climate. Set your phone to 'beep' you every few hours over the course of a week, and at each beep, ask yourself, 'What's my climate right now?' Map your changing climate over the week.

- Notice other people's climates, and even mass climates, and watch the connection between climates and events in people's lives and in the world at large.

- What does this mean for you?

CHAPTER 13

TEN SPIRITUAL AND PRACTICAL SECRETS FOR ATTRACTING WHAT YOU WANT

'The foolish man seeks happiness in the distance. The wise grows it under his feet.'

JAMES OPPENHEIM

I have been studying how our mind shapes our life since I was about 13 or 14 years old. I remember very clearly one day when I found myself standing on the top step at the back door of my parents' house, looking up at the sky and apologizing to God. I had a different idea of God from the one I had been taught at school, and I was feeling guilty about it. I thought it must be sin or blasphemy to think the way I was thinking, and thought I'd better apologize.

My thoughts then were much as they are now. And I intuitively felt that I could use the power of God to make my dreams come true if I just thought really hard about them and trusted that they would come true. Clear thought and belief were my simple formula.

My experiences as a teenager showed me in no uncertain terms just how true these intuitions were. I learned that my state of mind, what I focused on and whether I believed things could happen or not, played a considerable role, not only in defining how I responded *to* life events, but also in how I created them *for myself*.

The only downside was that I had some self-esteem issues that meant I rarely believed that I was worthy of having the things I really wanted. But I understood that it was my *expectation* of not getting what I wanted that was the cause of these apparent failures. It took me quite some time to reach a mental space where I could turn that around.

In the years since then I have studied much of what has been written about our ability to 'manifest' or 'attract' what we want. In this chapter I have fused the wisest lessons with my own intuitive and scientific understanding of the nature of reality, and added a few insights from my personal experiences, to create a list of both spiritual and practical secrets.

I have chosen the word 'secret' partly because many people interested in the subject have read the international best seller *The Secret,* or watched the documentary film, but also because I do feel that, while many of the tips I share are obvious when you really think about them, most people have little knowledge of them – they remain hidden from ordinary awareness like little secrets.

I hope you find something here that really works for you.

1. CHOOSE WHAT INSPIRES YOU

This is a pretty obvious secret when you think about it. Why would you choose a goal that didn't inspire you? The reason I include it as a secret is because of what it means. I believe that if something is right for you, then it will feel right to you, and you will be inspired by it. This feeling will often be information from Big You, which knows what's around the corner.

At the same time, it will be a presentiment. Your feelings will move back through time from the future to the present. This means it's your destiny in some ways. It's not set in stone, as we know, but the probability of it happening is high. This doesn't mean that you just have to sit down and wait, though! Part of life's journey is learning to create and achieve. But if the probability of something is high it does mean that if you commit to it then things will often line up for you. If it feels right then the deck will often be stacked in your favor, as it were.

I can relate this to many choices I have made in my own life. When I was in my final year of high school, even though I received 'unconditional offers' (I didn't need to pass any of my sixth-year exams, as I'd got good enough grades in my fifth year) for places at three leading universities, I turned them down and went with a less famous university, the University of Strathclyde, in Glasgow, which had made me a really tough 'conditional offer,' which basically meant that I'd have to work really hard and get even better grades in my sixth year than I had in my fifth. My friends thought I was mad! But going to the University of Strathclyde just felt like the right thing to do, even though I hardly knew anything about it.

It turned out to be the right university for me, not least because there were some excellent teachers there, and a professor who joined while I was in my second year, William J. Kerr, was without doubt one of the best teachers I had ever known. I learned a lot about the art of teaching and giving lectures from him.

But I think the main reason for my being at Strathclyde University was that I did my PhD in his research group. In my third and final year, due to a recruitment freeze by the major pharmaceutical companies, there was only a handful of jobs going in my field, and there must have been at least 500 students finishing PhDs around the UK who were qualified for them. But, as a rising star in the world of chemistry at the time, and with a growing reputation for producing first-class students, 'Billy' had won the trust of many big companies, so the students in our group were pretty much guaranteed interviews.

We had to stand on our own two feet at the interviews, of course, but the quality of the education we had received worked in our favor. It was no surprise that every single member of our PhD group was employed over that two-year recruitment freeze. One of my friends from that group has gone on to be a top chemistry professor himself.

I can't think of a job that was more perfectly suited to me than the one I got. It was a newly created post that normally had someone from a different field of chemistry in it, but the company wondered if an organic chemist would add a unique quality. The job exposed me to the broad field of drug development, where I learned all about the placebo effect. Four years later, when I left the pharmaceutical industry to pursue my dream of writing and speaking, I had a depth of understanding of how the mind not only shaped the chemistry of life, but also shaped the chemistry of the body, and was well equipped to write about the power of the mind to heal.

I encountered some very difficult financial times after my leap of faith, and if my dream hadn't inspired me, I doubt I'd have stuck it out. That's a key lesson I've learned: if something inspires you then you're more likely to stick it out, even when things get tough.

Even so, I almost went back into the pharmaceutical industry about four years later, but Elizabeth reminded me of how important my dream was to me and rekindled my determination to follow my heart.

That's probably why I unconsciously sabotaged myself in the final interview for a job I'd applied for. It was the last of three interviews I'd had that day for the post, and three senior people were in attendance. I was quite sure I was getting the job at that point, but it just felt so wrong to be back there.

So, when asked what my aspirations would be if I got the job, I found that the words that popped out my mouth surprised me and came out so fast that I wasn't able to put them back in again. I told them that I'd probably only stay in the role for 18 months to two years at the most, and would then use my skills to push upward until I got onto the board of directors. Two of the interviewers were nodding in agreement at this point, but then I added: 'Because, quite frankly, I don't care for your ethics! And neither do many of the public. As a future CEO, I'd bring it all back to being about saving lives and not about shareholder value.'

Those three men, who had previously been so keen on talking with me, began to shift uncomfortably in their seats. One of them stared at me as if he was trying to burn a hole in my head. I pretty much knew then that I hadn't got the job, but it didn't matter. Even though Elizabeth and I were broke at the time, and I had thought I needed the job, it just didn't feel right. Following my dream was what inspired me.

If you are inspired, you'll keep going.

2. WVA

Now that *is* a secret, because who knows what it means? It is a very practical one. It's a three-step dynamic process:

- **W**rite your goals down.

- **V**isualize them happening, or meditate on them regularly.

- **A**ct to make them happen.

Writing your goals down ensures that your mind is focused on what is really important in your life. I do this bit in two parts. The first part is to write down the goal. That's a no-brainer! But the second part is to write down a paragraph or two about why it is important. That makes sure that you really only pursue what is meaningful for you.

It's too easy to forget about goals when we don't do this. Believe me, I know. We get so caught up in our lives that other things take over. I have found that writing my goals down and explaining why they are important helps keep a clear intention, regardless of what else is going on in my life. In this way you use the three levels of creation not only consciously but also unconsciously.

I also find it is important to visualize, meditate, or reflect on goals regularly. Let's face it, life has a habit of throwing the odd curve ball from time to time, so I find that this helps me to stay inspired and focused, even as other things are happening in my life.

Research at the Dominican University of California in 2007 found that writing goals down and acting on them had a considerable impact on success.[1] The research involved 149 participants ranging from 23 to 72 years of age from many different backgrounds and countries. They were randomized into five groups. Group 1 was asked to *think* about goals they'd like to accomplish over the next four weeks, and also about the importance of each one, how difficult it might be, if they had the skills, etc. Group 2 was asked to write down their goals and consider the importance, etc., as Group 1 had. Group 3 went a little further. They wrote down their goals, considered their importance and made action commitments. Group 4 went a stage further still. Not only did they formulate action commitments, but they were also asked to send those commitments to a supportive friend. Group 5 went as far as to make weekly progress reports to the supportive friend.

Can you guess the outcome of the study? Yes, Group 5 achieved the most and Group 1 the least. In fact, Group 5 achieved 78 percent more than Group 1.

Accountability turns out to be very important. Telling a supportive friend about your commitments is more effective than keeping them to yourself, and it's better still to send your friend weekly progress reports. This is why life coaching is so powerful, because a good coach will often ask you to commit to something and follow through with it, and they will check up on you to make sure you actually did it.

The moral of the story? Write your goals down and act on them!

So, get clear on what you want, and make the time to write it down. If you can't make the time to write your goals down, how do you think you'll be able to find time to achieve them?

When I run seminars, after we do a goal-setting exercise, I impress upon the groups the importance of taking at least one action within three days. It's easy to feel pumped up at a seminar. Not only do you feel inspired by the teacher and the material presented, but you're surrounded by like-minded people who are highly supportive of your aspirations. But when you go back to your everyday life, your commitment to your goals often wanes.

To be really honest, I doubt that I would have resigned from the pharmaceutical industry after attending Tony Robbins' seminar in 1999 if I hadn't taken the action the very next day. If I'd left it for a few days I think my courage would have dissipated, and I'd have found reasons why it was a silly idea to leave a good job in pursuit of a pipe dream. I can tell you now, with the greatest possible sincerity, that after writing seven books and speaking in front of tens of thousands of people, I am glad I took that action!

3. YOU HAVE TO GIVE TO RECEIVE

I have found three ways in which you can benefit from this nugget of wisdom:

3.1. Giving Brings Abundance

Sounds counterintuitive, doesn't it? But giving is a statement of abundance. To give you must have, otherwise how can you give? I know that's fairly obvious. But what's not so obvious is the little trick it plays on the mind. Giving presupposes that you have something to give. So, with that sense of abundance – of 'I have' – dripping into your unconscious, you start to use the three levels of creation unconsciously to attract more of whatever it is you are giving. Opportunities then tend to present themselves that didn't seem to be available before.

Of course, since we're dripping stuff into the unconscious here, you have to give with *intent,* and not with the thought '*I hope this works. What if it doesn't? I've just bought a more expensive blouse. Oh no – if it backfires I'll be worse off. Maybe I should just take it back.* Then the act of giving isn't really saying 'I have,' is it? It's saying 'I don't have and I'll have even less now.'

So you need to judge for yourself when it is intelligent and appropriate to use this technique. Much depends upon your belief in it. Some people find it works well for small things, but that their belief wavers when it comes to bigger stuff.

3.2. Giving Yourself Brings Time, Happiness, and Love

The second way to use this secret is one that I personally like to use. It's the giving of yourself.

As above, giving in this way attracts more of what you've given. If you are generous with your time, for example, you will find that you have more time to be generous with. I have discovered that when I help people (within reason), even when I have deadlines to meet, my work becomes more creative and inspired than it was before, so the quality is better and I get along faster. At first this idea sounds counterintuitive too, because you're more focused on *losing* time, but if you put that thought aside and help because it's the right thing to do, you *gain* time.

Putting this idea into practice might mean that you give your time, or your patience, your undivided attention, your forgiveness, your compassion or your love. Giving any of those things seems to bring more of them into your life. If you want to be loved more, then love more! It's a very simple but extremely empowering idea. It's a real secret, too, because few people outside those who study psychology or personal development will have any idea of it.

A real side effect is that in helping those to whom we're connected, we help everyone, and therefore ourselves, because we are so connected through our social networks.

The Harvard social network research that I described earlier,[2] where happiness and depression were proven to be contagious throughout a social network, also found that one of the ways of helping a depressed person was to introduce them to your group. Each new social contact a person gained had a net positive impact upon their emotional state, so the more connected the network became, the happier overall it became.

Helping others helps yourself. I guess it's proof of the old adage that 'what goes around comes around.'

3.3 Giving Thanks Brings More to Be Thankful For

The third form of giving is giving thanks – gratitude. This is probably the most powerful, as it can have far-reaching positive consequences. I personally rank gratitude exercises as some of the best of all the self-help techniques that I have ever learned.

For a start, gratitude makes us feel happier. Research comparing people who were asked to count their blessings with those who counted their hassles (which most people do) found that those counting their blessings were 25 percent happier after the experiment than the hassles group.[3]

Gratitude also improves our relationships. The divorce courts are littered with the corpses of relationships where one partner took the other for granted. It's quite common to forget the great stuff about the people close to us because after a while we pay so much attention to the little annoyances instead. But one of the wisest things I've ever learned is that what you pay attention to affects your emotions. If you focus on stuff that bugs you, you'll find more stuff like that, and your emotions will be on a downward spiral, at least until something breaks, you go to sleep, or something positive happens. The mind is pretty clear-cut that way. Gratitude helps you pay attention to what's important and your emotions move in an upward spiral. Your happiness, contentment, and relationships improve as a side effect.

I can recommend two powerful gratitude exercises:

- The first is a daily exercise where you write down 5–10 things that you're grateful for that have happened in the last 24 hours. You can just think of the things if you like, but I've found that it works really well to make a 'Gratitude Journal' and fill it with all the blessings you count.

- The second is what I call 'Pick a Person.' This is where you spend 5–10 minutes a day thinking about all the reasons why you are grateful for a particular person being in your life. You pick a different person every day, from your loved ones to your friends, your work colleagues, to your postman.

4. POSITIVE EMOTION SPEEDS THINGS UP; NEGATIVE EMOTION SLOWS THINGS DOWN

This is another of those quite obvious observations, but despite the fact that it's so obvious it doesn't seem to stop people using it to frustrate their attempts to achieve what they want!

When you get stressed and frustrated because things aren't working out, you only prolong the agony. Since like attracts like, you just get more stressed and frustrated – again until something breaks, usually a blood vessel! Even worse, from this state you faithfully use the three levels to create more of what you're focusing on: the fact that you don't have what you want. Staying relaxed, positive, and hopeful, on the other hand, seems to cut through whatever is obstructing you.

Here's how it works. I like to think of our intentions as creating little vibrations and our emotions as making them bigger. Whatever the emotion, the intention is amplified. Now, on the one hand you have the desire for what you want and on the other you have the negative emotions you're feeling about not getting it. So the energy associated with what you don't want is stronger than the energy associated with what you do want. So what do you think you're going to get?

The rule is that whichever side the stronger emotion is on is what you will get.

Now if you think of your goal in a positive way, the stronger emotion will be on that side of the equation, and you will get – or at least move toward – what you want.

I have found that states like excitement, enthusiasm, passion, curiosity, and fascination all seem to help me move toward what I want. They are strong forms of positive emotion that can sometimes cut through the chaff of frustration when things aren't going the right way.

All of this can feel like a bit of a catch-22 of sorts – the only way to change things appears to be not to let the situation bug you, but if it doesn't bug you, why change it at all? I wrestled with this apparent paradox for years when I was in my teens and early 20s. With the self-esteem issues I mentioned earlier, I often wanted something then thought there was no way I could get it, and the frustration that created pushed what I wanted away from me. I ended up feeling that I needed to not want something in order to get it. But I really did want it. So, what's the solution?

I have found that your state of mind is all-important. Learning to complain less is a winner, especially if you do a lot of it – and a lot of people do a lot of complaining! It's a habit, even for those who think they don't complain. I have challenged numerous 'I never complain' people to take the 21-day Complaint-Free Challenge,[4] which is where you need to go 21 full days without complaining, moaning, criticizing, or unfairly judging a person or a thing. You keep track by moving a wristband to the other wrist every time you complain.

Most of the 'I never complain' people soon realize that they actually complain a lot more than they think they do. On average, the first day they wear their band they have to switch it about ten times, and that's just in the first couple of hours.

It's actually an excellent training program. It's like going to the gym for your mind and emotions. It especially helps you to spend less time focusing on what you don't want and more time focusing on what you do want.

Another way I've found to increase positive emotion and reduce negative emotion is laughter. I love watching comedy on TV or at the cinema. The sitcom *Friends* is one of my favorites. I also love *Frasier* and *The Big Bang Theory*. In the UK, I laugh at chat-show hosts Graham Norton and Alan Carr. In the USA, Ellen DeGeneres is one of my favorite chat-show hosts. I love to laugh, and it certainly puts me in a positive mood.

I am also a secret fan of 'Oor Wullie' and 'The Broons,' two comic strips published every week in Scotland's *Sunday Post*. I have several 'Oor Wullie' and 'The Broons' books at home and almost always have one at the side of my bed. I find that a few minutes of their light-hearted comedy is the ideal recipe for a peaceful night's sleep.

A third way of increasing positive emotion is gratitude, which I've already covered in the third secret.

5. MAKE COURSE CORRECTIONS – IDENTIFY AND CHANGE FALSE BELIEFS

This is something that I do a lot. It's probably the self-help exercise that I've done more than any other, and it has facilitated some considerable transformations in my life. I have evolved my own process, one that really works for me.

Throughout our lives we are inevitably faced with challenges, but, as we know, they offer us the opportunity to grow. Many of them require us to look inside ourselves to see how our own thoughts, emotions, and beliefs correlate with the situations we are faced with. When we change the thoughts, emotions, and especially the beliefs, then we correlate with a different experience, and so life changes to line up with our new ideas. Then we can emerge from the challenge as a (consciousness-) expanded version of ourselves.

When I first started out on my new career as an author and speaker I was actually holding myself back. It wasn't intentional. I had aspirations. But I had a false idea in my mind – a belief – that associated success with being away from home so often that I'd never see my family. This is some people's experience, and on some level I took it on board as an inevitable outcome if I was successful.

The desire to spend lots of quality time with my family was so strong that I would then sabotage myself. This often took the form of a lack of confidence; feeling and acting small around people who were authority figures, or who could be important in my career. Even though I wanted to be confident, the belief that if I succeeded I wouldn't see my family caused me to act in such a way that I wouldn't succeed. So confidence deserted me at these seemingly important times. It was frustrating, because I just couldn't seem to be at my best when I needed to be.

Once I identified that belief and questioned it, I was able to change it. I realized that career success didn't have to equate to a lack of family time. I could mold what I did in a way that suited me. I reasoned that with success came greater financial resources, so I could live where I wanted to live, and I could travel to see family when I wanted to, and even pay for them to come to me. I reminded myself that I could call the shots in my life. It was then that my career world started to look a lot brighter. It was only a false belief that had held me back.

Beliefs are like invisible internal forces that pull you in particular directions. It's really great when your beliefs are healthy and have you seeing the world in a positive light. Then you often find that life presents you with numerous blessings. People without those beliefs think you're just lucky. But when your beliefs aren't healthy, or when they're restrictive, it's best to change them. Changing beliefs is really just like making a little internal course correction. Once you make the correction your life lines up in the direction you want it to move in.

Here's a simple process I use to identify and change beliefs. I call it 'the cross-examination technique' (well, Elizabeth actually gave it that name after she used it effectively):

- Write everything down – from what the situation is that pains you to how you really feel about it. Don't hold back!

- Pick holes in what you've written with the intention of identifying false beliefs. Ask yourself questions like, 'Why do I believe that?' and 'What does that say about me?' and write down your responses. This isn't a five-minute exercise – allow yourself the time to really think about your answers.

- It's sometimes useful to ask yourself, 'What's the payoff that I get from things being as they are?' You need to be willing to be totally, brutally honest with yourself at this stage. You'll start to arrive at ideas (beliefs) about yourself, about other people, about your worthiness, about whether you deserve happiness – stuff like that.

- Now cross-examine what you've written. Look at your statements about yourself and the beliefs you've identified. From the mindset of a willingness to change, ask yourself:

  - Is this belief/statement absolutely true? Can I honestly say that it is really, 100 percent true?

  - Why isn't it true?

  - If it isn't true, what would be true?

- Write your answers down. Your third answer is your opportunity to write down a new and empowering belief. It should be a statement of how you choose to see yourself, others, your life, or the world from now on.

- Finally, repeat the new belief with intent (really state it as a fact) 20 times a day – 10 times in the morning and 10 in the evening – until you feel that you don't need to any more. You'll know when this is because you'll feel completely different, and aspects of your life will have changed for the better.

6. AFFIRMATIONS

There's a slight crossover here with beliefs in that an affirmation is an affirmative statement about something. At the end of the belief exercise, your new belief is an affirmation.

Affirmations are handy for helping us to adopt new mindsets or beliefs. Regularly repeating them helps them to take root deep in your consciousness.

I personally use affirmations a lot. One of my all-time favorites is:

*I live each day with happiness and joy,
trusting that only good things come to me.*

You don't need to believe an affirmation totally when you first state it. But this is where their power comes in. As you repeat them, your thinking, your emotions, and even circumstances around you begin to change to reflect the affirmation you are making. Your reality begins to confirm it. So, even though you didn't believe it at first, you do now because it is now true in your life.

Everyone makes affirmations, even though they might not think they do. 'I'm no good at this' – whatever 'this' might be! – is an affirmation. A better one would be: 'Even though I make some mistakes, I am getting better at this.' With that affirmation you will probably find yourself getting better at whatever it is and enjoying it more.

Everything we tell ourselves about ourselves, about others, and about the world on a regular basis is an affirmation. It's handy if yours are positive and you see goodness in people and in the word. But if you see problems everywhere and find fault with everyone, then it would be wise to change what you tell yourself because your life might faithfully reflect this.

One person in a workshop responded to this idea with, 'But I'm just stating a fact.' I replied, 'Are you?' Facts are sparser than you might think. Most of what we call facts are opinions – interpretations of events. They are *not* facts. But as long as you believe they're facts they will be facts for you. Your affirmations about them will make that happen.

My personal experience of affirmations is that they are subtle yet powerful direction-changing tools. Repeating them is like paddling a few strokes to set yourself on a different direction. It's almost effortless because you make affirmations anyway, every day of your life. So all you're really doing now is changing the direction you're pointing your boat in.

Here are a couple of suggestions to help you get started:

- How about changing 'This is terrible – I'll never do it, I'll never get better, I'm stuck here' to 'I will find a way. There's always a way. I love that I am good at finding solutions to problems. I can do it.'

- How about changing 'That person is nasty and horrible' to 'I wonder if that person is experiencing some personal difficulties in their life that are causing them to behave the way they're behaving?'

And here are a few positive ones that can set up your day:

- 'I am grateful for all that I am, for all that I have, and for all that I experience.'

- 'I love and accept myself just as I am.'

- 'I have the inner strength to handle any situation I find myself in.'

- 'I am flexible. I welcome change in my life and adapt with courage and ease.'

- 'I allow myself to feel happiness and joy for no reason at all – simply because I deserve it!'

7. PATIENCE – A WATCHED POT NEVER BOILS

We've all heard that patience is a virtue, but probably few of us have actually thought about it. It's just something we say. But I have found it to be extremely important in creating the things we want. Without patience, we tend to think about what we want so much that we end up paying more attention to the fact that it's not happened yet. And you know what that's going to result in, don't you?

Patience is a take on the spiritual ideas around detaching from the outcome or going with the flow. I sometimes refer to it as the old adage 'a watched pot never boils' to make the point. It's when we detach our minds from the fact that what we want hasn't happened yet that things begin to flow for us again.

I shared this nugget of wisdom at a seminar once and a woman just burst out laughing. At first I thought I'd said something funny. I have a tendency to do that at times when I'm giving a talk, but usually it's on purpose. When I asked her what was up, she said it was the sudden realization of what she had been doing, and that she was just so relieved that she had an answer that she couldn't help laughing.

Of course the other seminar attendees and I now needed to know more. She explained that she'd recently left a successful corporate career to set up her own business as a corporate coach and trainer. She had been really nervous about it, but her thought was that it was now or never, so she had courageously taken the plunge.

She had invested in some PR and managed to get a few small pieces in the local media that told a bit of her story and advertised her services. But she was terribly worried that if she didn't pick up any clients she'd have lost money and would be on a road to failure.

Unfortunately, she said, that was her dominant thought, and as a result she was so worried about getting clients that she had been checking her e-mails literally every five or 10 minutes all through the last few days. How many of you reading this can relate to that? Of course, she now realized that doing that wasn't going to work out so well.

The group suggested that she didn't check her e-mails at all on Monday (the seminar was on a Saturday), and she agreed that that's what she would do. She reasoned that it might be good if she didn't immediately respond to people anyway. It might create the perception that she was busy.

I received an e-mail from her a couple of weeks later. She had been so busy working with her new clients that she hadn't had time to write before. Not only had she not checked her e-mails on the Monday, she hadn't checked them on the Tuesday either. When she had logged in on the Wednesday morning, she had been thrilled to find a number of e-mails asking about her services and it had all taken off from there.

Patience isn't always easy. It takes practice. But if you do practice it with the intent of developing it then you will find it easier. Here's a nice affirmation that might help you to focus on this goal:

I am patient in my life.
I live in the moment and I trust that
good things are flowing toward me.

8. UPS AND DOWNS ARE NORMAL

Yes, really. When things seem to stop working or take a nosedive, it's really easy to feel that you've failed, done something wrong or not done enough, but downs have a habit of accompanying ups, and it's just the cyclic way that things work.

Remember that nature and the cosmos are cyclic. As our biology is in synch with many of those cycles, and our biology influences how we think and feel, it is only natural that we seem to find our lives are cyclic as well. With this in mind, we can start to appreciate why the ascent to the heights of our goals is unlikely to be in a straight line.

With this understanding, you don't need to assume you're doing something wrong whenever you have a 'bad' day. You may just need to have a bit of patience or make a course correction by challenging some of your beliefs. I do both of these things.

Also, if you have your mind focused on a goal, then the ups and downs will result in a net upward direction. There will come a time when you're experiencing a 'down,' but you'll realize that you're actually in a much better position than you were when you were in an 'up' a few months earlier.

If you can get to a place where you're OK with this idea, you'll see difficulties as challenges and not as problems. And in my experience, *that* makes all the difference.

Let's illustrate this by taking a quick look at my personal journey. After I resigned from my job in the pharmaceutical industry, the next few months were definitely a high, but downs occurred when I realized that hardly anyone was coming to my talks and seminars, and I ran out of money. Later in the year a few friends and I cofounded a charity. That began an up for me. But in the middle of my two-year period as a director of the charity there was a big down because we ran out of money and most of the volunteers left. We reorganized and picked up again, culminating in a nine-day, 24-event peace festival – another up. But after that it was a down again, as I went bankrupt.

There was an up when I started writing my first book. It was a rewarding experience. Things went down, though, because I was unable to get a job to earn any money. Then I got a few teaching jobs – up again – but was turned down by every publisher I contacted (down).

At this point it was clear that, even though I had been rejected by publishers, I had still written a book. Even though the rejection was hard to take and definitely felt like a down, I was in a much better place than I'd been before I started writing the book. I'd had plenty of ups and downs, but the trajectory was in an upward direction. And then I self-published the book and went up again.

I could go on – but you get the point! Ups and downs are definitely normal.

If you do feel really stuck at any time and patience is hard, then try making a course correction. Belief work is always a rewarding experience. That's what I do!

9. IF YOU REALLY CAN'T CHANGE SOMETHING, CHANGE YOURSELF

This secret is one of the wisest things I've ever learned in my life, and given that growth seems to be the nature of consciousness, I think it is the underlying point of many of the pickles we get ourselves into.

As I've already stated, I believe we are evolving toward a more spiritual way of living – toward more love, empathy, compassion, and kindness. With that in mind, almost every moment in life is offering us something – an opportunity to rise up and become more than we were previously.

A few years ago my understanding of this point reached a new high. I was listening to a talk in London by Wayne Dyer, and he invited a woman named Immaculée Ilibagiza onto the stage. She was a survivor of the 1994 Rwandan holocaust in which over a million of her tribe, the Tutsi, were massacred.

She described how she hid in a very small bathroom in the local pastor's home with seven other women throughout the 91 days of the massacre. They barely ate because the pastor had to be really careful not to give others in the household the impression that he was feeding Tutsis. Such an 'offense' would have meant certain death for him and his family. As a consequence, the women lost half their body weight.

Immaculée was terrified at first, then distraught as she learned of the fate of her parents and some of her brothers. But then she began to pray. She prayed for many hours each day, asking for help with forgiveness.

When the massacre was finally over and the UN was in charge of the country, Immaculée and several others had the opportunity to visit some of the ringleaders of the massacre in prison. The prison guards encouraged the survivors to take some revenge by spitting, kicking, or hurling abuse at the prisoners.

Immaculée was confronted with the leader of the gang who had killed her mother and her dear brother Damascene:

> [He] was sobbing. I could feel his shame. He looked up at me for only a moment, but our eyes met. I reached out, touched his hands lightly, and quietly said what I'd come to say: 'I forgive you.' My heart eased immediately, and I saw the tension release in [his] shoulders.

She recounts her full story in her powerfully moving book *Left to Tell*.[5]

In the talk she gave in London, she explained that there are times in life when there really isn't anything you can do to change the situation so you only have one option – to change yourself. That is what she did: she became forgiveness!

Few of us are in situations as severe as Immaculée's, but we can still use our challenges as opportunities to be more compassionate, confident, patient, understanding, forgiving, good at negotiating, a better parent, etc. Years later, when we reflect on our life, we may realize that was the whole point.

10. IT'S ALL ABOUT LOVE

One of the most important things I have ever learned is that it's not necessarily what you do in life that's important, it's how you do it. Whatever you do, do it with empathy, do it with compassion, do it with kindness, do it with honesty, and do it with love. That's success in my book.

All of us are looking for peace and happiness. But we won't find what we're looking for outside ourselves, only inside. OK, I know it can be quite annoying when people remind us to look within. I remember a time about ten years ago when I was having coffee with my friend Ailsa. She was going through a challenging time, and I was about to offer her my pearls of wisdom. I think she sensed what I was about to say, because she said, *'If one more person tells me to look within, I'm going to punch them.'* I took that as my cue to keep my mouth shut.

Looking within actually was the solution, but I think the annoying element to that piece of advice is that it is often offered by people with little real knowledge of what it actually means, and the recipients somehow know that.

But if you really do want to find happiness, well… there are many ways to look within. Apart from identifying and changing beliefs, I find that the most powerful is simply to ask yourself, 'Who am I being right now in my response to this situation?' Are you *being* frustration, anger, or judgment, for instance? Now that you are aware of what's inside you, you can change it.

What to change it to? My advice is to choose love. That might be expressed in your mind or as a practical act, but when you choose love, empathy, compassion, understanding, forgiveness and kindness, things change around because *you* have changed.

The peace and happiness that you've been looking for are found in that simple choice, and through it you come to understand that you are the master of your own destiny. No matter what happens around you, you can always choose love.

Many great teachers throughout history have offered us this wisdom, but we haven't always listened. One of the most powerful examples of it was shared by Viktor Frankl, who survived the Nazi concentration camps during the Second World War. In his deeply moving book *Man's Search for Meaning*, he wrote:

> *We who lived in concentration camps can remember the men who walked through huts comforting others, offering their last piece of bread. They may have been few in*

number but they offer sufficient proof that everything can be taken from a man but one thing: the last of the human freedoms. The right to choose one's attitude in any given set of circumstances, to choose one's own way.[6]

Some of you may be familiar with these words. They've been repeated by hundreds of motivational speakers for decades and can be found on thousands of web pages. But there's a reason for that: the wisdom is breathtaking in its power.

The question is, are we ready to finally listen to these words?

Ask yourself right now: 'Can I choose love more in my life?' If you can, ask yourself, 'How?'

Now do it!

CHAPTER 14

SOME FINAL THOUGHTS

'At the touch of love everyone becomes a poet.'

PLATO

I am always conscious when discussing our capacity to create what we want in life that some people blame themselves when things turn out badly for them. So I'd like to address this now.

BLAME AND RESPONSIBILITY

I am hopeful that by now you will have realized that although we have choices, we are influenced by other forces. It's not *all* down to us. Often things happen that are not a product of our thinking, emotions, or beliefs. Our plans don't always work. We can't always shape our physical reality. The only choice we *always* have is who we're going to be in any given set of circumstances.

Of course there are times when events don't appear to be a product of our minds, but on closer investigation we realize our beliefs have increased the likelihood of them occurring. I have experienced this on a number of occasions. Seemingly unexpected things happened that didn't appear to have anything to do with me, but to be honest they were a good fit for the shape of my mind. It wasn't conscious, but my beliefs were definitely calling the shots.

But it would be wrong to blame myself for these occurrences. I didn't choose to have those beliefs. I learned many of them as a child, through stuff I'd read or seen on TV, and through my interpretation of life events. So, if you feel your beliefs have led to unwanted events in your life, don't blame yourself for what has happened. What matters is what you do now.

Some people have difficulty here because they believe that they need to accept responsibility for their past in order to change things. Then, in accepting responsibility, they blame themselves. It can be hard to disentangle the two.

The ideal solution is to accept responsibility that you have beliefs that have resulted in you being in a difficult place, but also accept that you didn't know what they were. Then you can change things.

There's a more obvious matter regarding responsibility. Is an 18-year-old who is constantly in trouble with the police completely to blame for his actions? The justice system would say yes, but what if he was neglected as a child? This has considerable detrimental effects on the structural development of the brain. The first two years are crucial. I wrote a chapter on this in my book *Why Kindness Is Good for You*, which I'd encourage you to read if you want a deeper exploration of how emotional environment impacts brain growth.[1] Specifically, if an infant is neglected, the orbitofrontal cortex (the part of the brain behind the orbits of the eyes), which is involved in the ability to exercise free will, develops holes, or areas with less neural wiring than they should have. This means that when the infant grows up into a young adult, they don't have the brain capacity to be as in control of themselves as people who were brought up surrounded by love. The net result is that our delinquent teenager doesn't have the same free will as you and I do. He doesn't have the same capacity to control his behavior, and it's even harder for him if he has grown up in an environment where he has seen crime everywhere.

A study which compared the brains of 41 murderers who had pleaded not guilty by reason of insanity with the brains of 41 ordinary people found that the murderers had extremely underpowered regions of the prefrontal cortex, as well as an imbalance between the left and right orbitofrontal cortex and the prefrontal cortex.[2] In particular, the left was less developed than the right, which incidentally is the side associated with compassion. The murderers had less capacity to feel positive emotions, but greater capacity to feel negative emotions. The scientists pointed out that the brain differences could result in aggression and lack of self-control.

I'm left wondering if more emphasis needs to be placed on treating brain deficiencies with psychological techniques rather than locking so many people up. Our society doesn't have the resources for this at present, but maybe if we accepted the need then we could take steps in that direction. This isn't about letting people off the hook, but recognizing that there are neurological consequences of upbringing in a number of people which, coupled with the wrong type of environment, can increase the probability of violence.

Maybe as we shift in our societies over the next few generations there will be fewer children brought up in unfair conditions, and we will see a collective shift toward less crime and punishment.

DEPRESSION

Another area where people blame themselves is depression. Some mothers who experience post-natal depression blame themselves for not being responsive to their children, or because on some occasions they can't even bear to hold their baby. But it is *absolutely* not their fault. They don't choose depression. It is something that happens.

My mum developed post-natal depression in 1976 after the birth of my youngest sister, Lynn. Due to improper understanding and ineffective treatment, it lasted for many years and gave my mum the idea that it was her own fault that she wasn't feeling right. She felt that she should be more in control of herself and was in fact advised to 'give yourself a shake.' That was well intended, but expecting someone with depression to shake themselves out of it is like expecting a person with a broken leg to just run it off.

I experienced depression myself in 1994 and 1998. In 1998 it lasted for about six months, and I vividly remember coming home from work every day, pulling the curtains shut, lying on the floor, and having a cry. Depression is no picnic, and it feels almost impossible to snap out of it. It is a miracle to me that my mum got through the years of post-natal depression to be the kind and compassionate person she is today. It is testimony to her great inner strength.

Some studies into post-natal depression have shown that it can result from a deficiency of EPA in the brain. EPA is an omega-3 fatty acid that you can get from oily fish. A fetus needs it for the growth of its brain, and if the mother's diet isn't rich in it then the fetus will take what it needs from the mother's brain. After the birth the mother's brain can lack EPA and depression can result. The late David Servan-Schreiber, clinical professor of psychiatry at the University of Pittsburgh School of Medicine, explained this very well in his excellent book *Healing without Freud or Prozac*.[3]

So, if you are depressed, it's not your fault and you shouldn't blame yourself. The important thing is that you get the right help and support.

You might wonder if things were always meant to be this way. Maybe they were. Perhaps depression was always a likely branch on your tree of probable life. If so, then the experience will have been there for a reason, which you may or may not understand at the moment.

'SOUL GROWTH' CONDITIONS

I would also like to address another subject that comes up frequently when I discuss creating your own reality. With so much written about the law of attraction nowadays, some people mistakenly believe that people in poverty-stricken countries are somehow at fault for their situation, especially if they believe that thoughts become reality.

I cannot stress enough how much I don't accept this idea. But I do accept that if Big You is real and does see the whole canvas, there might be a reason for a person being born into those conditions. I can only speculate, but there may be a reason in terms of the soul's growth, or it might even involve showing the rest of us the appalling state of affairs we are still permitting in our seemingly advanced world. In some ways, part of the reason may be to educate the rest of us in empathy and compassion.

The person living in those difficult conditions would have no idea of this and would certainly not accept that they chose their circumstances. And they didn't. I didn't personally choose my life in the sense that I have any awareness of it. We are born with no knowledge of our greater existence at all, at least I wasn't, or I certainly don't remember it. Maybe it's different for other people.

If you look at life in this way then the beginnings are definitely mapped out. At that point the hand of destiny reigns supreme. We are born into choices already made. There is nothing we can do about that. Choice is only available to us later in life. And the degree of choice will always depend on the environment. A person living in poverty and famine has much less choice than probably every single person reading this book. The current of destiny is far stronger for them throughout their lives, unless their circumstances change, perhaps because we as a global community have got off our bottoms and have said, *'This cannot go on any longer.'*

These people's circumstances are not their fault. They just do not have the same opportunities as those living in environments where life is much less mapped out, and the tree of probable life has many more branches, offering much more chance to pursue hopes and aspirations.

We're not all the same. What applies to one doesn't always apply to another, so we should resist the temptation to assume everyone has the same ability to shape their life. Much of what has been written about the law of attraction applies to a great number of people in the world, but is meaningless to billions of others.

THE FORMULA OF DESTINY

Enough of the blame, now for some fun! I love mathematics – sad, I know – and I've often wondered if destiny and free will could be reduced to a simple equation. I have spent many moments lost in thought, doodling in the notebook I purchased in the last few days before the end of the year, grouping together the seeming forces of destiny and trying to marry them up with free will and intention, and, if you can bear with me, I'll present an equation of sorts:

$$Reality = Mind \times Forces\ of\ Destiny$$

There! Simple, isn't it?

You could always write it as R=MD, if you wanted to be fancy, where R is reality, M is mind, and D is forces of destiny.

You might wonder what the point of this is. Actually, it's just a way of grouping together forces that work together.

I've already shown that your intention is affected by your emotions and beliefs, so these group together as M (mind). And there are also multiple forces at play, from cosmic cycles to genetics to the inspirations of Big You and the entanglement between soulmates. I've just lumped all these forces together as D, forces of destiny. If you did want to fit them all in, then the equation would have the following quantities in it:

Reality that you experience is proportional to Intention (I), Emotion (E), Beliefs (B), Momentum of current experience (p), External Forces (Fe), Internal Forces (Fi), Other people's influences (O), and anything else I haven't thought of (X). Or:

$$R \propto IEBpFeFiOX$$

I've included momentum of current experience (the math symbol for momentum is a small 'p,' so I've kept with this) because it's common sense that when we make choices in life we don't just immediately walk into a new life – there is always carry-over. It's like trying to turn a ship in the ocean. The captain might turn the rudder to steer to the left, but the ship still goes forward for a bit. Life is much like this too.

As for the rest of the equation, external forces are cosmic forces and other forces in nature, while internal ones include genetics as well as influences and connections in the fabric of reality. Other people influence us too, of course, so that's factored in as well and also encapsulates collective mental and emotional climates. And I'm very conscious of the fact that I don't have all the answers, so I've added 'X' as other forces.

The bottom line is that we can't disentangle our mind from our reality, but we aren't independent of the forces acting upon us either. Life really is like being on a small boat on a wide river, with currents flowing continuously and the wind blowing from time to time. We have a nice paddle and are born with the ability to paddle wherever we want. We might think we are doing precisely that, but actually we are drifting slightly with every current we paddle through. But we are always choosing which direction we are heading in.

Some people think our thoughts are predestined, but as long as we feel that we're choosing, it makes no difference – it's just a philosophical argument. If I believe I'm choosing then that's good enough for me. And I take comfort in the idea that we're all moving toward more love and a deeper experience of interconnectedness. When I make choices that help us get there, I feel better inside.

WHAT NOW?

But I'm aware that some people would like a more definite answer than that. The title of this book is *Is Your Life Mapped Out?* To ask the question presupposes that there is either a 'yes' or a 'no' answer. But it seems that it is *and* it isn't. The seeming confusion is that there is more than one map. Each map, or branch of the tree of probable life, has its own destin(y)ation, just as each branch of a tree reaches out to a different point in the sky, but our choices move us from one branch to another.

There are undoubtedly some branches that are thicker and more probable than others, and some people are likely to be born with a stronger sense of destiny or purpose than others. Life might be more mapped out for them. There is always a high probability that they will make the choices needed to get to a 'pre-intended' destination. But we are never forced to make these choices. Some just seem more obvious than others, and so some people seemingly live out a destiny that always seemed to be on the cards.

In each moment, life is more about probabilities than certainties. We do sense what is ahead of us from time to time, and some people might therefore feel that the future is predestined, but sensing that future gives us the option to stay on the branch we are on or choose a different branch. In this way, free will is dominant over destiny. Life is *not* mapped out!

But neither do we live on a blank canvas. We don't make it all up as we go along. It is not 100 percent one or the other, as the question presupposes. We were born at a time that was right for us, and there is always a pull from the future. Free will is in our choices whether to follow or not and, most importantly, what kind of person we're going to be in any given moment.

When faced with a difficult person, for instance, we can choose to act with compassion or dismissal. No matter what happens in life, no matter who is around us and what situations we find ourselves in, we can always choose how we respond. The bigger choices aren't always easy – they can take real courage. But they are there for the taking, and the situations facing us are there because we are capable of meeting them as a higher version of ourselves. If that weren't the case then we wouldn't be where we are.

Regardless of whether there is an ultimate physical destiny or not, the deeper destiny is spiritual. It is our ascent to *being* more love, empathy, compassion, and kindness. In the broadest sense, that *is* mapped out. How we get there, though, is up to us.

******

So, you see, it's not easy to give a definitive 'yes' or 'no' to the question of whether life is mapped out or not. It really depends upon your perspective. I'd say that it is not, but that there is a destination that we will all arrive at eventually and so that is mapped out. For me, that is the real journey in life.

Where are you now on that journey, and what kind of person are you? It is quality of character that matters most.

Many seek peace as an ultimate goal. Martin Luther King once said, '*Peace is not merely a distant goal that we seek, but a means by which we arrive at that goal.*' We can experience peace by letting go of things needing to be any way other than the way they are right now.

Sounds simple, doesn't it? The idea *is* simple, but putting it into practice is the hard part. It can be difficult to let things be as they are, but maybe try it out from time to time. Start with the little things. Let people around you be who they need to be. Don't judge them, but accept that they are on a journey just as you are. Then you might find that you see them with fresh eyes and, dare I say, even appreciate them.

As we let things be, we may find the flow of life takes us to where we need to be, just when we need to be there. We are led to accept that everything is as it needs to be.

These are very spiritual ideas, and many people feel torn between living them and trying to change things that are not working. They flit from spiritual to practical and back to spiritual and then to practical again. Is there a way to marry the two?

There is. It is trusting in what you are moved to do. Inspiration comes from Big You, which has a bigger perspective. So, if you feel moved to use your skills to bring about change, be it in your locality or even globally, then go for it. Perhaps that's the most probable branch on your tree of probable life. It's what you came here to do, and you can do it in any way you like. If you do it with empathy, with compassion, with kindness, with love, you help all of us. That's your choice, of course. But I'd say that love *is* the point.

Love is all around because it's a key aspect of consciousness. We know this deep in our hearts. It's why so many love songs are written, and why just about every movie ever made has a love story in it. I think it's time we really started listening to this message. Love is *everywhere*. It's in the story of our lives, it's in the relationships we have with our pets, it's even in the way that governments govern. Governments are people after all, and most are really just trying to find solutions to the world's problems. We might not agree with what they do, but that's up to us and we have the democratic right to exercise our choices on that stage.

Love is even in the atoms right in front of your face. Zip, there goes a particle of love whizzing right past you. Did you feel it? Just take a breath with that thought and you *will* feel it. Go on, try it now. Stop what you're doing and breathe in the love. You're always doing it. You always have been. You just haven't always noticed.

When you do notice, life takes on a miraculous new tint. A miracle, after all, is just a shift in perspective!

Are you ready to shift? The destiny of the world awaits your decision...

Chapter 1: Chronobiology

1. http://en.wikipedia.org/wiki/Circadian_rhythm

2. http://en.wikipedia.org/wiki/Linnaeus%27_flower_clock

3. http://en.wikipedia.org/wiki/Chronobiology

4. http://en.wikipedia.org/wiki/Menstrual_cycle

5. http://en.wikipedia.org/wiki/Melatonin

6. http://en.wikipedia.org/wiki/Period_(gene)

7. http://en.wikipedia.org/wiki/CLOCK

8. http://en.wikipedia.org/wiki/Suprachiasmatic_nucleus

9. G. Figueiro and M.S. Rea, 'Lack of short-wavelength light during the school day delays dim light melatonin onset (DLMO) in middle school students,' *Neuroendocrinology Letters*, 2010, 31(1), 92–6

10. S.P. Law, 'The regulation of menstrual cycle and its relationship to the moon,' *Acta. Obstetricia et Gynecologica Scandinavica*, 1986, 65, 45–8. See also E. Friedman, 'Menstrual and lunar cycles,' *American Journal of Obstetrics and Gynecology*, 1981, 140(3), 350

11. A. Cagnacci, R. Soldani, G.B. Melis, and A. Volpe, 'Diurnal rhythms of labor and delivery in women: modulation by parity and seasons,' *American Journal of Obstetrics & Gynecology*, 1998, 178(1), 140–45

12. F.A. Brown Jr, 'Persistent activity rhythms in the oyster,' *American Journal of Physiology*, 1954, 178, 510–14

13. N.A. Buckley, I.M. Whyte, and A.H. Dawson, 'There are days… and moons. Self-poisoning is not lunacy,' *Medical Journal of Australia,* 1993, 159(11–12), 786–9

Chapter 2: Written in the Stars

1. http://en.wikipedia.org/wiki/Solar_cycle

2. http://en.wikipedia.org/wiki/Geomagnetic_storm

3. www.spaceweather.com

4. http://www.pbs.org/wgbh/nova/nature/magnetic-impact-on-animals.html

5. M. Klinowska, 'Cetacean stranding sites relate to geomagnetic topology,' *Aquatic Mammals*, 1985, 1, 27–32. For a further link between geomagnetic disturbances and whale navigation and strandings, see also:

   M. Klinowska, 'Cetacean live stranding dates relate to geomagnetic disturbances,' *Aquatic Mammals*, 1986, 11(3), 109–19

   M.M. Walker, J.L. Kirschvink, G. Ahmed, and A.E. Diction, 'Evidence that fin whales respond to the geomagnetic field during migration,' *Journal of Experimental Biology*, 1992, 171, 67–78

6. T. Ritz, P. Thalau, J.B. Phillips, R. Wiltschko and W. Wiltschko, 'Resonance effects indicate a radical-pair mechanism for avian magnetic compass,' *Nature*, 2004, 429, 177–80

7. T. Kimchi and J. Terkel, 'Magnetic compass orientation in the blind mole rat *Spalax ehrenbergi*,' *Journal of Experimental Biology*, 2001, 204(4), 751–8

8. J.A. Etheredge, S.M. Perez, O.R. Taylor and R. Jander, 'Monarch butterflies (*Danaus plexippus* L.) use a magnetic compass for navigation,' *Proceedings of the National Academy of Sciences*, 1999, 96(24), 13,845–6

9. K.J. Lohmann and C.M.F. Lohmann, 'Detection of magnetic field intensity by sea turtles,' *Nature*, 1996, 380, 59–61. Other animals use the Earth's magnetic field for navigation too. The following is a short list of some articles of interest:

   'Migratory songbirds have a specialized night-vision brain area' in http://www.sciencedaily.com/releases/2005/05/050523234717.htm

'Chickens orient using a magnetic compass' in http://www.sciencedaily.com/releases/2005/08/050825071055.htm

'Pigeons can sense the Earth's magnetic field; ability might allow them to return home' in http://www.sciencedaily.com/releases/2004/11/041129100043.htm

'Lobsters navigate by magnetism, study says' in http://news.nationalgeographic.com/news/2003/01/0106_030106_lobster.html

N. Banks and R.B. Srygley, 'Orientation by magnetic field in leaf-cutter ants *Atta colombica* (Hymenoptera: Formicidae),' *Ethology*, 2003, 109, 835–46

10. R. Robin Baker, *Human Navigation and Magnetoreception* (Manchester University Press, Manchester, 1989)

11. Michael Persinger stimulated the brain's temporal lobes using the now famous 'God helmet.' For information, see http://en.wikipedia.org/wiki/God_helmet. It is my contention that magnetic fields impact the brain and facilitate different receptivity to the fields of consciousness that permeate all of nature. The 'perceived presence' reported by many who wear the helmet might then be an awareness of consciousness or presences around the users who are more receptive to them under the presence of the magnetic fields.

12. D.R. Belov, I.E. Kanunikov, and B.V. Kiselev, 'Dependence of human EEG spatial synchronization on the geomagnetic activity on the day of experiment,' *Russian Journal of Physiology*, 1998, 84(8), 761–74

13. R.W. Kay, 'Geomagnetic storms: association with incidence of depression as measured by hospital admission,' *British Journal of Psychiatry*, 1994, 164, 403–9. See also P. Semm, T. Schneider, and L. Vollrath, 'Effects of Earth-strength magnetic field on electrical activity of pineal cells,' *Nature*, 1980, 288, 607–8

14. M. Berk, S. Dodd, and M. Henry, 'Do ambient electromagnetic fields affect behaviour? A demonstration of the relationship between geomagnetic storm activity and suicide,' *Bioelectromagnetics*, 2006, 27, 151–5

15. http://www.frbatlanta.org/pubs/wp/working_paper_2003-5b.
cfm?redirected=true (last accessed July 7, 2012)

16. For research showing effect of geomagnetic storms on the heart,
see:

Y.I. Gurfinkel, V.L. Voekov, E.V. Buravlyova, and S.E. Kondakov,
'Effect of geomagnetic storms on the erythrocyte sedimentation
rate in ischemic patients,' *Critical Reviews in Biomedical
Engineering*, 2001, 29(1), 65–76

D.A. Pikin, I. Gurfinkel, and V.N. Oraevskii, 'Effect of geomagnetic
disturbances on the blood coagulation system in patients with
ischemic heart diseases and prospects for correction with
medication,' *Biofizika*, 1998, 43(4), 617–22. This paper also
showed that aspirin reduced the negative effect of the magnetic
storms.

R.M. Baevsky, V.M. Petrov, G. Cornelissen, F. Halberg, K. Orth-
Gomer, T. Akerstedt, K. Otsuka, T. Breus, J. Siegelova, J. Dusek,
and B. Fiser, 'Meta-analysed heart rate variability, exposure to
geomagnetic storms, and the risk of ischemic heart-disease,'
Scripta Medica (Brno), 1997, 70(4–5), 201–6

Y.I. Gurfinkel, V.V. Liubimov, V.N. Oraevskii, L.M. Parafenova, and
A.S. Iuriev, 'The effect of geomagnetic disturbances in capillary
blood flow in ischemic heart disease patients,' *Biofizika*, 1995,
40(4), 793–9

17. S. Chernouss, A. Vinogradov, and E. Vlassova, 'Geophysical
hazard for human health in the circumpolar auroral belt: evidence
of a relationship between heart rate variation and electromagnetic
disturbances,' *Natural Hazards*, 2001, 23(2–3), 121–35

Chapter 3: Written in Our Genes

1. David R. Hamilton, PhD, *Why Kindness Is Good for You* (Hay
House, London, 2010), Chapter 10, 'Why Babies Need Love'

2. J.H. Fowler and N.A. Christakis, 'Dynamic spread of happiness in
a large social network: longitudinal analysis over 20 years in the
Framingham Heart Study,' *British Medical Journal*, 2008, 337,

a2, 338, 1–9. See also David R. Hamilton, PhD, *The Contagious Power of Thinking* (Hay House, London, 2011), Chapter 14, 'Can You Catch Happiness?'

3. For epigenetic effects following the Dutch famine, see:

    L.H. Lumey, F.W.A. van Poppel, 'The Dutch famine of 1944–45: mortality and morbidity in past and present generations,' *Social History of Medicine*, 1994, 7(2), 229–46

    L.H. Lumey, 'Decreased birthweights in infants after maternal in utero exposure to the Dutch famine of 1944–45,' *Paediatric and Perinatal Epidemiology*, 1992, 6(2), 240–53. See also Nessa Carey, *The Epigenetics Revolution* (Icon Books, London, 2011), Chapter 5, 'Why Aren't Identical Twins Actually Identical?' and L.A. Pray, 'Epigenetics: genome, meet your environment,' *The Scientist*, 2004, 18(13), 14

4. Carey, op. cit., Chapter 6, 'The Sins of the Fathers'. See also J. Marlor, 'Grandfather made me what I am,' *The Daily Telegraph*, October 30, 2007, http://www.telegraph.co.uk/science/science-news/3312230/Science-Grandfather-made-me-what-I-am.html# (last accessed July 8, 2012)

5. For the research showing a four-generational effect on rat embryos exposed to environmental toxins, see:
    M.D. Anway, C. Leathers, and M.K. Skinner, 'Endocrine disruptor vinclozolin induced epigenetic transgenerational adult-onset disease,' *Endocrinology*, 2006, 147(12), 5,515–23

    M.D. Anway, A.S. Cupp, M. Uzumcu, and M.K. Skinner, 'Epigenetic transgenerational actions of endocrine disruptors and male fertility,' *Science*, 2005, 308(5,727), 1,466–9

    See also R.T. Zoeller, 'Endocrine disruptors: do family lines carry an epigenetic record of previous generations' exposures?' *Endocrinology*, 2006, 147(12), 5,513–14

6. S.L. Rutherford and S. Lindquist, 'Hsp90 as a capacitor for morphological evolution,' *Nature*, 1998, 396, 336–43

7.   R.A. Waterland and R.L. Jirtle, 'Transposable elements: targets for early nutritional effects on epigenetic gene regulation,' *Molecular and Cellular Biology*, 2003, 23(15), 5,293–300

8.   F. Lyko, S. Foret, R. Kucharski, S. Wolf, C. Falckenhayn, and R. Maleszka, 'The honey bee epigenomes: differential methylation of brain DNA in queens and workers,' *PloS Biology*, 2010, 8(11), 1–12

9.   http://www.nytimes.com/2010/11/09/health/09brain.html (last accessed July 8, 2012)

10. For information and references on how the orbitofrontal cortex of the brain grows almost entirely after birth, see:

     David R. Hamilton, PhD, *Why Kindness Is Good for You* (Hay House, London, 2010), Chapter 10, 'Why Babies Need Love'.

     Sue Gerhardt, *Why Love Matters: How affection shapes a baby's brain* (Routledge, East Sussex, 2004)

11. For research showing how enriching life experience and physical exercise can stimulate neurogenesis, see:

     G. Kemperman, D. Gast and F.H. Gage, 'Neuroplasticity in old age: sustained five-fold induction of hippocampal neurogenesis by long-term environmental enrichment,' *Annals of Neurology*, 2002, 52, 135–43

     L. Lu, G. Bao, H. Chen, P. Xia, X. Fan, J. Zhang, G. Pei, and L. Ma, 'Modification of hippocampal neurogenesis and neuroplasticity by social environments,' *Experimental Biology*, 2003, 183(2), 600–609

     See also David R. Hamilton, PhD, *How Your Mind Can Heal Your Body* (Hay House, London, 2008), Chapter 4, 'The Power of Plasticity'

12. Cited in S. Blakeslee, 'Placebos prove so powerful even experts are surprised: new studies explore the brain's triumph over reality,' *New York Times*, October 13, 1998, http://www.nytimes.com/1998/10/13/science/placebos-prove-so-

powerful-even-experts-are-surprised-new-studies-explore-brain.
html?pagewanted=all&src=pm (last accessed July 8, 2012)

13. J.A. Dusek, H.H. Out, A.L. Wohlhueter, M. Bhasin, L.F. Zerbini,
M.G. Joseph, H. Benson, and To. Liberman, 'Genomic counter-
stress changes induced by the relaxation response,' *PloS ONE*,
2008, 3(7), e2576, 1–8

Chapter 4: Sensing the Future

1. B.L. Fredrickson, 'The broaden-and-build theory of positive
emotions,' *Philosophical Transactions of the Royal Society London
B*, 2004, 359, 1,367–77. See also Barbara L. Fredrickson,
Positivity (Crown Publishers, New York, 2009).

2. David R. Hamilton, PhD, *The Contagious Power of Thinking* (Hay
House, London, 2011), Chapter 1, 'I Feel It from Your Face'.
See also Dacher Keltner, *Born to Be Good: The science of a
meaningful life* (W. W. Norton & Company, New York, 2009).

3. L.J. Standish, L.C. Johnson, T. Richards, and L. Kozak, 'Evidence
of correlated functional MRI signals between distant human
brains,' *Alternative Therapies in Health and Medicine*, 2003, 9,
122–8. See also:

L.J. Standish, L. Kozak, L.C. Johnson, and T. Richards,
'Electroencephalographic evidence of correlated event-related
signals between the brains of spatially and sensory isolated human
subjects,' *Journal of Alternative and Complementary Medicine*,
2004, 10, 307–14

J. Wackermann, C. Seiter, H. Keibel, and H. Walach, 'Correlations
between brain electrical activities of two spatially separated human
subjects,' *Neuroscience Letters*, 2003, 336, 60–64

Dean Radin *Entangled Minds* (Pocket Books, New York, 2006)

4. Rupert Sheldrake, *Dogs That Know When Their Owners Are
Coming Home: And other unexplained powers of animals* (Crown
Publishers, New York, 2000)

5. For a good book that thoroughly covers research into
presentiment and precognition, see Larry Dossey, *The Power of*

Premonitions: How knowing the future can shape our lives (Hay House, London, 2010)

6.   D.I. Radin, 'Unconscious perception of future emotions: an experiment in presentiment,' *Journal of Scientific Exploration*, 1997, 11(2), 163–80

7.   D.I. Radin, 'Electrodermal presentiments of future emotions,' *Journal of Scientific Exploration*, 2004, 18(2), 253–73

8.   R. McCraty, M. Atkinson, and R.T. Bradley, 'Electrophysiological evidence of intuition: Part 1. The surprising role of the heart,' *The Journal of Alternative and Complementary Medicine*, 2004, 10(1), 133–43

9.   R.W. Doherty, L. Orimoto, T.M. Singelis, J. Hebb, and E. Hatfield, 'Emotional contagion: gender and occupational differences,' *Psychology of Women Quarterly*, 1995, 19, 355–71. Note: The study was measuring 'emotional contagion' – the likelihood of 'catching' the emotions of others. It is also a fairly accurate measure of empathy. See also David R. Hamilton, op. cit., Chapter 6, 'Soaking Up Emotions'.

10.   S.J.P. Spottiswoode and E.C. May, 'Skin conductance prestimulus response: analyses, artifacts and a pilot study,' *Journal of Scientific Exploration*, 2003, 17(4), 617–41

11.   H. Klintman, 'Is there a paranormal (precognitive) influence in certain types of perceptual sequences? Part 1,' *European Journal of Parapsychology*, 1983, 5(1), 19–50

12.   'Is this REALLY proof that man can see into the future?' *Daily Mail*, May 4, 2007. Author not given.

13.   C.R. Wildey, 'Biological response to stimulus,' Master's degree thesis in Electrical Engineering, University of Texas at Arlington, 2001, http://lkm.fri.uni-lj.si/xaigor/slo/znanclanki/Wildey1.pdf (last accessed July 9, 2012)

14. H.E. Puthoff, 'CIA-initiated remote viewing program at Stanford Research Institute,' *Journal of Scientific Exploration*, 1996, 10(1), 63–76

15. R. Targ, 'Remote viewing at Stanford Research Institute in the 1970s: a memoir,' *Journal of Scientific Exploration*, 1996, 10(1), 77–88

16. http://www.biomindsuperpowers.com/Pages/CIA-InitiatedRV.html

17. http://en.wikipedia.org/wiki/Copenhagen_interpretation

18. http://en.wikipedia.org/wiki/Many-worlds_interpretation

19. I took 100,000 thoughts a day as an average from different estimates of how many thoughts we think. The actual number isn't really relevant, only the approximate ratio of how many were yesterday's thoughts. I conducted a quick analysis on my own thinking over an hour one morning and concluded that around 80–90 percent of my train of thought and the subjects I was thinking about were roughly the same as they had been the day before.

20. Quinn used term during an interview for the film *Choice Point* conducted at the University of Michigan in 2011; quoted in Harry Massey and David R. Hamilton, PhD, *Choice Point: Align your purpose* (Hay House, Carlsbad, 2012)

Chapter 5: The Three Levels of Creation

1. Robert Holden, PhD, *Success Intelligence: Essential lessons and practices from the world's leading coaching program on authentic success* (Hay House, Carlsbad, 2008), Part I, 'The Manic Society'.

2. http://en.wikipedia.org/wiki/Quantum_entanglement

3. S. Sherwood and C.A. Roe, 'A review of dream ESP studies conducted since the Maimonides dream ESP programme,' *Journal of Consciousness Studies*, 2003, 10(6–7), 85–109

4. Dean Radin, *Entangled Minds* (Pocket Books, New York, 2006)

Chapter 6: Mind–Reality Interactions

1. R.G. Jahn, 'The persistent paradox of psychic phenomena: an engineering perspective,' *Proceedings of the IEEE*, 1982, 70(2), 136–70

2. http://www.princeton.edu/~pear/experiments.html (last accessed April 11, 2012)

3. Ibid.

4. J.D. Reed, *The New York Times*, March 9, 2003, http://www.nytimes.com/2003/03/09/nyregion/so-just-what-makes-the-earth-move.html (last accessed May 23, 2012)

5. http://noosphere.princeton.edu

6. Quoted in Reed, op. cit. (last accessed May 2, 2012)

7. If you're interested in reading more on the subject and looking at the data for yourself, you can visit the project website at http://noosphere.princeton.edu.

8. A discussion of the PEAR data from September 11th, 2001, can be found at: http://noosphere.princeton.edu/exploratory.analysis.html (last accessed May 23, 2012)

9. H. Schmidt, 'PK effect on prerecorded targets,' *Journal of the American Society for Psychical Research*, 1976, 70(3), 267–91

10. E.R. Gruber, 'PK effects on prerecorded group behavior of living systems,' *European Journal of Parapsychology*, 1980, 3(2), 167–75

11. E.R. Gruber, 'Conformance behavior involving animal and human subjects,' *European Journal of Parapsychology*, 1979, 3(I), 36–50

12. Ibid.

13. Gruber 1980, op. cit.

14. W.J.J. Snel and P.C. van der Sijde, 'The effect of retro-active distance healing on *Babesia rodhani* (rodent malaria) in rats,' *European Journal of Parapsychology*, 1990, 8, 123–30

15. With Braud's 1993 research the 'p' value was not under 0.05 but the effect size was large, so this didn't mean it wasn't a true result, only that there *could have* been other factors involved.

16. W. Braud, 'Wellness implications of retroactive intentional influence: exploring an outrageous hypothesis,' *Alternative Therapies in Health and Medicine*, 2000, 6(1), 37–48

17. For Schmidt's time-displaced research on his own breathing rate, see: H. Schmidt, 'Random generators and living systems as targets in retro-PK experiments,' *Journal of the American Society for Psychical Research,* 1997, 91(1), 1–13

18. Dean Radin, *Entangled Minds* (Pocket Books, New York, 2006)

19. Braud 2000, op. cit.

20. L. Leibovici, 'Effects of remote, retroactive intercessory prayer on outcomes in patients with bloodstream infection: randomised controlled trial,' *British Medical Journal*, 2001, 323 (7327), 1,450–51

Chapter 7: When the Conditions Are Ripe

1. W. Braud, G. Davis, and R. Wood, 'Experiments with Matthew Manning,' *Journal of the Society for Psychical Research,* 1979, 50(782), 199–223

2. David R. Hamilton, PhD, *Why Kindness Is Good for You* (Hay House, London, 2010), Chapter 13, 'The Evolution of Kindness'

3. H. Schmidt, 'PK effect on prerecorded targets,' *Journal of the American Society for Psychical Research*, 1976, 70(3), 267–91

4. M.J. Schlitz and C. Honorton, 'Ganzfeld psi performance within an artistically gifted population,' *Journal of the American Society for Psychical Research*, 1992, 86, 83–98

5. http://www.dailymail.co.uk/sciencetech/article-452833/Is-REALLY-proof-man-future.html

6. T. Lawrence, 'Gathering in the sheep and goats: a meta-analysis of forced choice sheep-goat ESP studies, 1947–1993,' *Proceedings*

of the *Parapsychological Association 36th Annual Conference*, ed. M. J. Schlitz, 1993, 75–86

7. L. Casler, 'The improvement of clairvoyant scores by means of hypnotic suggestion,' *Journal of Parapsychology*, 1962, 26, 77–87

8. B.J. Dunne and R.G. Jahn, 'Consciousness, information, and living systems,' *Cellular and Molecular Biology*, 2005, 51(7), 703–14. The reference they quoted was 12, M. Ibison and S. Jeffers, 'A double-slit diffraction experiment to investigate claims of consciousness-related anomalies,' *Journal of Scientific Exploration*, 1998, 12, 543–50. See also R.G. Jahn and B.J. Dunne, 'The PEAR proposition,' *Journal of Scientific Exploration*, 2005, 19(2), 195–245

9. Rupert Sheldrake, *The Science Delusion* (Coronet, London, 2012)

10. Rupert Sheldrake, *The Sense of Being Stared At: and other aspects of the extended mind* (Arrow Books, London, 2003)

11. For Honorton and Ferrari's conclusion regarding four moderation variables, see C. Honorton and D.C. Ferrari, 'Future telling: a meta-analysis of forced-choice precognition experiments, 1935–1987,' *Journal of Parapsychology*, 1989, 53, 281–308

12. Ibid.

13. Ibid.

14. Ibid.

15. Ibid.

Chapter 8: Quantum Interconnections

1. A. Aspect, J. Dalibard, and G. Roger, 'Experimental test of Bell's inequalities using time-varying analyzers,' *Physical Review Letters*, 1982, 49, 1804–7

2. W. Tittel, J. Brendel, H. Zbinden, and N. Gisin, 'Violation of Bell inequalities by photons more than 10 km apart,' *Physical Review Letters*, 1998, 81, 3,563–6. Their preliminary experiment was: W. Tittel, J. Brendel, B. Gisin, T. Herzog, H. Zbinden, and N. Gisin,

'Experimental demonstration of quantum-correlations over more than 10 kilometers,' *Physical Review A*, 1998, 57, 3,229

3. Robert Nadeau and Menas Kafatos, *The Non Local Universe* (Oxford University Press, Oxford, 1999)

4. http://en.wikipedia.org/wiki/Wheeler%27s_delayed_choice_experiment

5. V. Jacques, E. Wu, F. Grosshans, F. Treussart, P. Grangier, A. Aspect, and J-R. Roch, 'Experimental realization of Wheeler's delayed-choice Gedanken experiment,' *Science*, 2007, 3,015, 5,814, 966–8. See also Adrian Cho, 'After a short delay, quantum mechanics becomes even weirder,' *Sciencemag*, February 16, 2007

6. http://www.abc.net.au/radionational/programs/scienceshow/the-anthropic-universe/3302686 (broadcast Saturday February 18, 2006, 12 p.m.)

7. http://people.ccmr.cornell.edu/~muchomas/8.04/Lecs/lec_FeynmanDiagrams/node3.html

8. Stephen Hawking and Leonard Mlodinow, *The Grand Design* (Bantam Press, London, 2010)

9. S. Jay Olson and Timothy Ralph, 'Extraction of timelike entanglement from the quantum vacuum,' Physics Review A, 2012, 85(1), 12,306. See also: http://www.wired.com/wiredscience/2011/01/timelike-entanglement/

10. For the Zeilinger research showing how entanglement could be established in the past, see X-S. Ma, S. Zotter, J. Kofler, R. Ursin, T. Jennewein, C. Brukner, and A. Zeilinger, 'Experimental delayed choice entanglement swapping,' *Nature Physics*, 2012, published online April 26, 2012

11. Ibid.

Chapter 11: Life Before Life and Life After Death

1. Cited in Raymond A. Moody, *The Light Beyond* (Rider, London, 2005). This book is also an excellent source of information for some of the scientific validation of life after death.

2. P. van Lommel, R. van Wees, V. Meyers, and I. Elfferich, 'Near-death experience in survivors of cardiac arrest: a prospective study in the Netherlands,' *The Lancet*, 2001, 358, 2,039–45

3. P. van Lommel, 'Near-death experiences: the experience of the self as real and not as an illusion,' *Annals of the New York Academy of Sciences*, 2011, 1,234, 19–28

4. Ibid.

5. Michael Sabom, *Recollections of Death: A medical investigation* (Harper & Row, New York, 1982)

6. Anita Moorjani, *Dying to Be Me: My journey from cancer, to near death, to true healing* (Hay House, Carlsbad, 2012)

7. Michael Newton, *Destiny of Souls* (Llewellyn Publications, Woodbury, 2000)

8. Professor Archie Roy, cited in Gordon Smith, *The Unbelievable Truth: A medium's insider guide to the unseen world* (Hay House, London, 2004)

Chapter 12: Collective Destiny – Where You Go, We Go

1. Harry Massey and David R. Hamilton, PhD, *Choice Point: Align your purpose* (Hay House, Carlsbad, 2012)

2. T.J. Scanlon, R.N. Luben, F.L. Scanlon, and N. Singleton, 'Is Friday 13th bad for your health?' *British Medical Journal*, 1993. 307(6,919), 1,584–6

3. S. Nayha, 'Traffic deaths and superstition on Friday 13th,' *American Journal of Psychiatry*, 2002, 159(12), 2,110–11

4. Cited in Dacher Keltner, *Born to be Good: The science of a meaningful life* (W. W. Norton & Company, New York, 2009)

5. J.H. Fowler and N.A Christakis, 'Dynamic spread of happiness in a large social network: longitudinal analysis over 20 years in the Framingham Heart Study,' *British Medical Journal*, 2008, 337, a2, 338, 1–9, and J.N. Rosenquist, J.H. Fowler, and N.A. Christakis, 'Social network determinants of depression,' *Molecular Psychiatry*,

2010, 1–9. See also David R. Hamilton, PhD, *The Contagious Power of Thinking* (Hay House, London, 2011).

6. Comment made on Monday June 18, 2012: http://news.sky.com/story/949887/burmas-aung-san-suu-kyi-honoured-in-ireland

7. Lao Tzu was a Chinese philosopher who lived in the sixth century BC and is believed to be the author of the *Tao Te Ching*.

Chapter 13: Ten Spiritual and Practical Secrets for Attracting What You Want

1. http://www.dominican.edu/academics/ahss/psych/faculty/fulltime/gailmatthews/researchsummary2.pdf (last accessed July 10, 2012)

2. J.H. Fowler and N.A. Christakis, 'Dynamic spread of happiness in a large social network: longitudinal analysis over 20 years in the Framingham Heart Study,' *British Medical Journal*, 2008, 337, a2, 338, 1–9, and J.N. Rosenquist, J.H. Fowler, and N.A. Christakis, 'Social network determinants of depression,' *Molecular Psychiatry*, 2010, 1–9

3. R.A. Emmons and M.E. McCullouch, 'Counting blessings versus burdens: an experimental investigation of gratitude and subjective well-being in daily life,' *Journal of Personality and Social Psychology*, 2003, 84(2), 377–89

4. http://www.acomplaintfreeworld.org/

5. Immaculée Ilibagiza, *Left to Tell* (Hay House, Carlsbad, 2007)

6. Victor Frankl, *Man's Search for Meaning* (Beacon Press, Boston, 1962)

Chapter 14: Some Final Thoughts

1. David R. Hamilton, PhD, *Why Kindness Is Good for You* (Hay House, London, 2010), Chapter 10, 'Why Babies Need Love'

2. A. Raine, M. Buchsbaum, and L. LaCasse, 'Brain abnormalities in murderers indicated by PET,' *Biological Psychiatry*, 1997, 42, 495–508

3. David Servan-Schrieber, *Healing Without Freud or Prozac* (Pan MacMillan, London, 2011)

JOIN THE HAY HOUSE FAMILY

As the leading self-help, mind, body and spirit publisher in the UK, we'd like to welcome you to our family so that you can enjoy all the benefits our website has to offer.

 **EXTRACTS** from a selection of your favourite author titles

 COMPETITIONS, PRIZES & SPECIAL OFFERS Win extracts, money off, downloads and so much more

 LISTEN to a range of radio interviews and our latest audio publications

 CELEBRATE YOUR BIRTHDAY An inspiring gift will be sent your way

 **LATEST NEWS** Keep up with the latest news from and about our authors

 ATTEND OUR AUTHOR EVENTS Be the first to hear about our author events

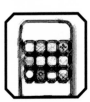 **iPHONE APPS** Download your favourite app for your iPhone

 HAY HOUSE INFORMATION Ask us anything, all enquiries answered

join us online at **www.hayhouse.co.uk**

  292B Kensal Road, London W10 5BE
T: 020 8962 1230 E: info@hayhouse.co.uk

ABOUT THE AUTHOR

Photographer: Stephen Mulhearn

David R. Hamilton gained a first-class honours degree in chemistry, specializing in biological and medical chemistry, and a PhD in organic chemistry. After graduating in 1995, David spent four years working for one of the world's largest pharmaceutical companies, and also served as an athletics coach and team manager for one of the UK's top athletics clubs. He left both roles in 1999. In 2000 he cofounded Spirit Aid Foundation, an international relief charity helping children whose lives have been affected by war and poverty. In 2002, as a director of Spirit Aid, he helped produce a 9-day, 24-event festival of peace in Glasgow. He served as a director of Spirit Aid until the end of 2002. From 2004 until 2005, he taught chemistry and ecology at James Watt College of Further and Higher Education, and tutored chemistry at the University of Glasgow.

In 2005, he self-published his first book, *It's the Thought That Counts*, which was published by Hay House in 2006. David is now the author of seven books, all published by Hay House. He has been featured on TV and radio and been the subject of numerous national newspaper articles. He spends most of his time writing, giving talks, and leading workshops. David also writes a regular blog for The Huffington Post

www.drdavidhamilton.com

CPSIA information can be obtained at www.ICGtesting.com
Printed in the USA
BVOW081608180912

300725BV00002B/2/P